What others are saying about this book:

"Very well written and informative. It is excellent for new and experienced teachers. We always need guidelines and to have all this information in one book is helpful." — Christine DiSisto, Teacher, Stormville, NY

"This is a well thought out, well organized guide." — Andrea Guillet, Teacher, Raleigh, NC

"Stress is a given in the teaching profession. This book not only acknowledges its existence, it provides valuable information on how to prevent it! As an experienced 25-year teacher, I would include this book in my must-have home library as a practical guide in preventing and dealing with stress in my career."
— Shelley Levine, Teacher, New York, NY

"It is nice to read a book with lesson planning, time management, and discipline strategies all in one!" — Kathy Buscher, Teacher, South Portland, ME

"A thoughtful and comprehensive approach to dealing with stress. Should help a lot!" — Martin Levinson, L.C.S.W., Psychiatric Social Worker, St. Louis, MO

7 Steps to Stress Free Teaching
The stress prevention planning guide for today's teachers

7 Steps to Stress Free Teaching

A Stress Prevention Planning Guide for Teachers

Lisa Burke

EDUCATORS'
LIGHTHOUSE

Published by:
Educators' Lighthouse
5133 Fairmead Circle
Raleigh, NC 27613

Printed in the United States of America.

Publisher's Cataloging-in-Publication Data
(Provided by Quality Books, Inc.)

Burke, Lisa (Lisa Maria), 1967-
      7 steps to stress free teaching : a stress
   prevention planning guide for teachers / Lisa Burke
   -- 1st ed.
      p. cm.
      Includes index.
      LCCN: 98-93946
      ISBN: 0-9668233-5-4
      1. Teaching. 2. Stress management.   I. Title.
   II. Title: Seven steps to stress free teaching
   LB1027.B87 1999   371.102
                          QBI98-1586

Limits of Liability and Disclaimer of Warranty
The author and publisher have designed this book to provide information in regard to the subject matter covered. It is sold with the understanding that the publisher and author are not engaged in rendering medical, legal, or other professional services. If medical, legal or other expert assistance is required, the services of a competent professional should be sought. Every effort has been made to make this book as complete and as accurate as possible. However, the author and publisher make no warranty of any kind, expressed or implied, with regard to any and all of the information contained in this book. The author and publisher shall have neither liability nor responsibility to any person or entity with respect to any loss or damage caused, or alleged to be caused, directly or indirectly, by the information contained in this book.

If you do not wish to be bound by the above, you may return this book to the publisher for a full refund.

Acknowledgments

This book could not have become a reality without all of the lessons I have learned from the many fine educators I have had the privilege to meet, to speak, and to work with over the past several years. I would especially like to thank Diana Agius, Janice Bloom, Kathy Buscher, Karen Coats, Maggie Davis, Christine DiSisto, Rhoda Friedman, Charlotte Floyd, Andrea Guillet, Melanie Iversen, Richard Johnson, Shelley Levine, Marty Levinson, May Tilghman, Joanne Tritto, and Nancy Wujek for their invaluable feedback. I would also like to thank my editor, John Simone of Three Pyramids Publishing, and my graphic designer, Ingrid Beckman of DesignMill Graphic Design Studio, for all of their help. In addition, I would like to thank all of the librarians at the Wake County Public Library System and at the North Carolina State University libraries, D.H. Hill Library and Learning Resources Library, for their assistance.

Grateful acknowledgment is also made to the following people who have allowed me to use the words of other authors who said it so well that I could not say it better myself:

- Addison Wesley Longman, Inc. for permission to reprint information on pp. 65-66 from *Beyond Student Teaching* by Ellen Kronowitz ©1992 by Longman Publishing Group.

- Charles C Thomas, Publisher, Ltd. for permission to reprint information on p. 230 from *A Teacher's Guide to Classroom Management* by Elbert M. Hoppenstedt ©1991 by Charles C Thomas, Publisher, Ltd.

- Jossey-Bass Inc. Publishers for permission to reprint information on p. 61 from *Crisis in Education: Stress and Burnout in the American Teacher* by Barry Farber ©1991 by Jossey-Bass Inc. Publishers.

- Lippincott Williams & Wilkins Publishers for permission to reprint information on p. 14 and p. 26 from *Stress without Distress* by Hans Selye, M.D. ©1974 by Hans Selye, M.D.

- Barbara Scaros of the Edith Winthrop Teacher Center of Westchester for permission to reprint information on p. 7 and on pp. 12-13 from *Sight on Sites: An Approach to Coping with Teacher Stress—Preventing Burn-out* by Barbara Scaros ©1981 by the New York City Teacher Centers Consortium.

- State University of New York Press for permission to reprint information on p. 95 and on p. 129 from *Becoming an Effective Classroom Manager: A Resource for Teachers* by Bob F. Steere ©1988 by the State University of New York. All rights reserved.

My deepest gratitude goes out to my family, especially to my parents and to my brother, for their unending support. A special thank you goes to my husband for believing in me. His constant encouragement kept me going, even when *I* could not see the light at the end of the tunnel.

This book is dedicated to all teachers who want to be their best.

Contents

Chapter 1

Stress:
What You Need to Know

Are You "Stressed Out"?

Teachers, are you feeling "stressed out"? Ask yourself the following questions to find out:

- Do you feel excessive pressure from not having enough time to do the things you need to do?

- Are you leaving work frustrated and exhausted?

- Do you suffer from sleeping difficulties such as insomnia?

- Do you find it difficult to let go of work at the end of the day?

- Do you frequently experience gastro-intestinal problems such as ulcers, indigestion, or poor appetite?

- Do you experience low self-esteem or feelings of hopelessness?

- Do you feel as if you are in a long, dark tunnel without a light in sight?

If you can answer "yes" to one or more of the above questions, you might be experiencing some stress. If you are, take heart. You are not alone, and you *can* prevent it. This book shows you how.

Everyone experiences stress. But what exactly is stress? How can it be prevented?

Stress: What It Is

Stress is a physiological condition. Dr. Hans Selye, M.D., a leading scientist on stress, defines stress as "the nonspecific response of the body to any demand made upon it." According to Selye, "nonspecific" means that the body responds with the same physiological process regardless of the type of demand placed on it, pleasant or unpleasant. This response includes the release of cortisol and adrenaline into the system. As a result, blood pressure rises and heart rate increases. In addition, muscles tense, senses heighten, and metabolism changes. The demands on the body that trigger this physiological response are called stressors.

Stressors can be either internal or external events. They can also be physical or emotional. Examples include extreme heat and cold or the death of a loved one. Stressors disrupt a body's natural balance, and as a result, the body responds with stress.

General Adaptation Syndrome

For all kinds of stressors, the physiological response is the same. Selye named this response the "general adaptation syndrome." According to Selye, the general adaptation syndrome has three stages: alarm, resistance, and exhaustion.

In the first stage, you become more alert and your body poises for "fight or flight." This occurs whether the situation warrants this type of response or not. This response is left over from our evolutionary past where it was designed to protect us from the dangers experienced in our struggles for survival. The alarm stage is still very useful to us, especially when a stress response is needed for a short period of time, such as in the face of extreme danger. However, most modern stressors occur over a sustained period of time. As a result, the body stays primed to react and the alarm response stage spills over into the next stage—the stage of resistance.

In the resistance stage, your body uses energy to adapt to the stressor. The length of this stage depends upon the intensity of the stressor and your ability to adapt to it. If your body can adapt to the stressor, it returns to a state of natural balance. If the stressful situation is never dealt with, the long, severe stress eventually depletes your energy and decreases your body's resistance to the stressor. As the stressful situation continues, it leads to the third stage—mental, emotional, and physical exhaustion.

Positive and Negative Stress

The general adaptation syndrome can have a positive or negative trigger, or stressor. As a result, it can create positive or negative stress in your body. Positive stress is good. It helps motivate you. You need a certain amount of stress for peak performance. However, negative stress can be harmful.

Negative stress can make you feel anxious, nervous, depressed, and irritable. It can also decrease your patience and tolerance, affecting your interpersonal relationships. Moreover, it can affect your immune system and lead to health problems such as high blood pressure, migraine headaches, heart attacks, ulcers, and insomnia. If not dealt with, negative stress eventually leads to the state of mental, emotional, and physical exhaustion mentioned above. In this state, you often experience low self-esteem and feel hopeless, helpless, and weary. This state is often referred to as burnout.

Negative stress, or distress, is the type of stress that plagues most people. Distress is the focus of this book. It will be implied every time the word "stress" is used.

What we know about stress and its causes has great implications for all people, especially for those who experience it often.

Stress and Teaching

The American Institute of Stress has found that being a teacher is one of the most stressful occupations. In one study, it was found that some teachers experience more stress than police officers, miners, air traffic controllers, and even medical interns! This is not news to the millions of teachers of the world.

Time and time again, studies have found that teachers report some of the highest levels of occupational stress. High occupational stress is usually caused by physical danger, extreme pressure, or responsibility without control. The teaching profession can have all of these things. For most teachers, however, the cause of their high level of occupational stress is not an infrequent, intense event, such as those a firefighter might experience, but the cumulative effect of constant, subtle daily stressors involving danger, pressure, and responsibility without control.

Throughout history, teachers have experienced stress. This stress has traditionally been caused by the pressures of accountability, the constant change characterized by the profession, and the loneliness of the job. However, the culture and the educational system of a time period determines which unique stressors exist. As times change, so do some of the stressors.

A True Story While growing up, I do not remember having many new students join my classes in the middle of the school year. However, today I live in a community that is growing and changing rapidly. Dozens of real estate transactions occur daily. As a result, each year I have about a half dozen new students join my classes at different points during the school year. Each child becomes a new personality, a new need, and a new stressor for me. Although the change becomes easier to handle with each new student, I recognize that it is not a stressor that was common to my teachers when I was attending school.

Stressors

For today's teachers, there are three major categories of stressors: organizational, environmental, and individual.

- **Organizational stressors:**
   found in the work place, including the job itself and relationships with colleagues, administrators, and students.

- **Environmental stressors:**
   originate outside the work place, such as the students' families, community, or town, and the teacher's own family and friends.

- **Individual stressors:**
   include personal characteristics, such as personality type, attitude, and state of physical health.

This book focuses on organizational stressors and on those environmental and individual stressors related to the teaching profession.

What is Causing Your Stress?

Use the "Stress Inventory" on page 13 to find out which stressors are present in your life. This inventory helps you to identify your stressors, who or what is involved in them, where they occur, how often they occur, how much control you feel you have over the stressor, and how you currently deal with the stressor. Copy the table into a notebook that can also be used to complete the questions in the rest of this book (see the section "How to Get the Most Out of This Book" on page 16 for more information). Provide as many lines in your table as needed.

To help you complete the inventory, use the following questions as a guide.

- **Stressor**: What events cause you stress?
- **Who/What**: Who or what is involved in each stressful event? Is it a particular student, colleague, administrator, or parent? Is your own family involved? Are you the only person involved? Are your teaching materials, textbooks, computers, or other equipment involved? Write the name of the persons or things that is involved in each stressful event.
- **Where**: Where does each stressor occur? Does it occur at home, at school (such as the classroom, the teachers' lounge, the main office, the playground, and so forth), on the telephone, or some other place? Specify exactly where each one occurs.
- **Frequency**: How often does each one occur? Is it always, often, or seldom?
- **Amount of Control**: How much control do you *feel* you have over each event? Is it a high level of control, some control, or no control?
- **Coping Strategies**: How do you currently deal with each stressor? Do you get depressed, frustrated, or angry, or do you just laugh it off? Do you enlist the support of others? Specify exactly what you do in each event.

Stress Inventory

Stressor	Who/What	Where	Frequency	Amount of Control	Coping Strategies

Look at the stressors you identified. Are any related to your job? Can you group your stressors in any way? Are there any common elements among some or all of your stressors? Which stressors or group of stressors are contributing most to your stress?

Compare your list with what today's teachers find to contribute most to their stress: time management issues; student discipline problems; relationship tensions with administrators, colleagues, parents, and community members; inadequate resources; role conflict; and role ambiguity. Do some or many of your stressors fall within these categories? If yes, this book is here to help!

In this inventory, you have also identified the amount of control you feel you have over the stressors and the way in which you currently deal with the stressors. This important information is used later in this chapter.

Handling Stress

Even though many teachers are under a great deal of stress, it has been found that over two-thirds of teachers today say they would again choose the same career! This is a sign of dedication. For me, it is a calling.

A True Story It began in high school when I volunteered to be a reading tutor for younger students. Although my interest in teaching grew, I did not consider it as a career choice. Instead, I decided to join corporate America. When I found work unsatisfying, I began to teach part-time at a community college and volunteered my time to work with local middle school and high school students. My work with young people was very fulfilling. I felt whole. I knew then that I had found my calling.

Since most teachers plan on staying in the teaching profession, the skills needed to handle stress must be learned and mastered. However, teacher preparation programs usually focus on technical skills, not on stress management or stress prevention skills. You need these skills! Without them, your teaching effectiveness decreases and you might experience burnout. In addition, a lack of these skills has been found to contribute to teacher absenteeism and attrition. As a result, it is imperative that you learn how to handle and prevent stress.

Why Stress Prevention?

Stress management is handling stress after it has occurred. Its purpose is to mitigate the stress, not to prevent it from happening again. It is not easy coping with stress, and removing it is difficult. Stress management takes a lot of time, energy, and self-discipline.

In contrast, stress prevention takes a proactive, direct approach to stress. A review of research on coping with stress found that a direct approach aimed at improving stress prevention skills was more effective in dealing with stress than those approaches aimed at reducing or managing the experience of stress after it had occurred. There is an old saying that states, "An ounce of prevention is worth a pound of cure." Since a teacher does not have a lot of extra time and energy to spend on stress, prevention is the key.

Psychological and Emotional Responses to Stressors

Stress is not external to us. It is an internal response to a stressor. Although the internal physiological response is the same for all stressors, your psychological or emotional response varies depending upon the stressors. For example, one stressor scares you while another stressor frustrates you. The different responses depend upon your perceptions of these stressors.

In addition, different people can have different psychological and emotional responses to the same stressor. For instance, a stressor might cause you to become depressed while it might cause your friend to become anxious. These differences in reactions are attributed to your individual perceptions of the same stressor.

How you perceive a stressor determines whether your body responds with stress or your body stays in its balanced state. Therefore, the root of these perceptions need to be understood before stress can be successfully prevented.

Beliefs: The Root of Stress

Perceptions are determined by beliefs. When you believe that you have no control over a stressor, you perceive it as harmful, irritating, or threatening to your body's balance. As a result, your body responds with stress. Research shows that people who feel in control at work feel less stress than those who do not feel influential in their work environment. Therefore, you experience stress when you believe a stressor is out of your control.

Revisit your stress inventory. How much control do you feel you have over each of your stressors? If you feel you have only some control or no control over some of them, they are probably the stressors causing most of your stress.

Influences on Your Beliefs

Beliefs are influenced by conditioning factors, internal (such as age or sex) or external (such as parental influences, diet, or drugs). As a result, your conditioning factors color your perceptions of different stressors. This explains why you and your friend might have totally different reactions or different degrees of stress to the *same* stressor.

Conditioning factors also explain how you can have different stress reactions to *similar* stressors. In your stress inventory, you might have also found that you have different psychological or emotional reactions to similar stressors. For example, you might have a different reaction to two different classroom parents, even if you have identified or grouped both parents as similar stressors. You might feel nervous when interacting with one parent and irritated when interacting with the other. This happens because each stressor possesses unique characteristics. As a result of your conditioning factors, you react differently to each parent's unique characteristics, resulting in a slightly different psychological or emotional stress response.

Although each of us is influenced by unique conditioning factors and our stressors have unique characteristics, research has found many common elements among teachers' stress inventories. These elements form the foundation of chapters two through eight.

Teachers Can Prevent Stress

Yes, fellow teacher, you *can* prevent stress! Everyday you face countless stressors. If you feel you have only some or no control over the stressor, you will probably experience stress. However, if you feel you have control over it, you will have less stress. The good news is that teachers *do* have a higher degree of control over most of their stressors than they might believe.

Many teaching related stressors are situations that you, the teacher, *can* control. Even if the situation seems totally out of your control, there is usually some aspect of it that can be controlled.

You might be asking, "But how do you accomplish this? How do you know what can be controlled?" The skills needed to identify potential stressors and to implement stress preventative measures can be developed and nurtured by asking the right questions. This book provides these questions.

A True Story It was a year from hell. Everything seemed wrong. Most of the time I felt angry, frustrated, and exhausted. I felt stressed. When it was finally over, I wanted to find out if my terrible experience was the result of being in the wrong place at the wrong time or it was the result of something I did. I found out that most teachers experience a horrible year at some point in their careers. Many experience more than one. Knowing this, "Why me?" turned into "Why us?" and I began to search for answers. From my search, it became evident that teachers *can* prevent stress. Common threads emerged, and the steps for preventing a stressful year became apparent. I then contacted teachers from all over the country and found they were interested in my research. With their tremendous encouragement and support, I share my findings in this book.

How to Get the Most Out of This Book

This book's purpose is to help you, the teacher, prevent stress. It does this by helping you take control over many of the stressors found in teaching. In each of the seven steps that follow, questions help you develop stress prevention skills and strategies.

In order to get the most out of this book, it is important to thoroughly answer all of the questions in each of the seven steps. You need a notebook to record your answers. For some of the questions, existing school documents might have the answers. Keep these in a folder near your notebook so that you can easily refer to them as needed. You also need to have your lesson plan book or this book's companion lesson plan book, *7 Steps to Stress Free Teaching Plan Book*, for *Step 5: Create a Plan*. This companion resource is available from Educators' Lighthouse. Ordering information is provided on the last page of this book.

The seven steps to stress free teaching are:
- *Step 1: Take Care of Yourself*
- *Step 2: Understand the Expectations*
- *Step 3: Know Your Resources*
- *Step 4: Determine the Goals*
- *Step 5: Create a Plan*
- *Step 6: Implement and Assess the Plan*
- *Step 7: Reflect*

Take Care of Yourself, Understand the Expectations, and *Know Your Resources, Step 1* through *Step 3,* respectively, build a foundation needed for proactive stress prevention. *Step 4: Determine the Goals* and *Step 5: Create a Plan,* put a stress prevention structure in place. *Implement and Assess the Plan* and *Reflect,* steps six and seven, respectively, help ensure stress prevention success.

Remember, it is all the little steps we take that allow us to make great strides. So, let's begin with our first step, *Take Care of Yourself.*

Summary

In this introductory chapter, you learned what stress really is—a physiological response to a stressor in your environment. Stressors are demands placed on the body that trigger this response. In teaching, stressors are usually situations where you feel low levels of control. Your stress inventory helped you identify which stressors were causing most of your stress. The rest of this book helps you prevent the stress caused by those stressors which are related to teaching.

Chapter 2

Step 1:

Take Care of Yourself

For *preventing* stress, this step is key. Its focus is to make sure your personal needs are met. The following is an outline of what you will learn in this chapter.

The most important part of preventing stress is attending to your physical, mental, and emotional health. As a teacher, it is very easy to place your personal needs behind the needs of others. Without providing time and energy to take care of your health, stress continues to build. Eventually, you might experience burnout. To prevent this from happening, set boundaries to help create the reenergizing time needed for maintaining good health.

Second, understand the administrative details of your employment. For example, understand your contract's terms, and be aware of the criteria which is used to evaluate your teaching performance. This prevents misunderstandings between you and your employer, as well as the stress associated with them.

Third, provide opportunities for your personal and professional growth and renewal. Personal and professional growth and renewal strengthens self-esteem and helps to improve teaching skills. Opportunities for growth and renewal include continuing formal education, obtaining a mentor, and becoming active in professional associations.

Finally, help others. Helping others solve their stress related problems also helps you relieve your own stress. Therefore, identify where and when you can help other teachers and actively do so.

Step 1: Take Care of Yourself is very important because it lays a solid foundation on which to build a stress free teaching experience. Therefore, make sure this step is done completely and done first!

Health

Good health is a prerequisite for preventing stress. It helps your body function at its optimum level. Without health, stress can wear out your body and soul, weaken your teaching performance, and degrade your personal effectiveness.

Before analyzing what is needed for good health, you must first build in the time to maintain a healthy and balanced lifestyle. It must be scheduled! To find time, you might have to learn to say no to extra commitments, both work and non-work related. If you, like many teachers, tend to put others' needs before your own, stop! You *must* make the time to take care of your health for peak performance. The first question in this book deals with this issue because it is *the* most important factor in preventing stress.

Take out your notebook. Answer the following questions completely. To help you stay organized, the questions' first digit corresponds with the step number in the chapter title.

> 1.1 What can you do to ensure you have enough time for the following things?
>
> a. getting enough rest
>
> b. eating balanced meals
>
> c. exercising aerobically
>
> d. spending time with family and with those whom you care about
>
> e. growing spiritually
>
> f. exploring hobbies and non-work related interests
>
> g. exploring personal career growth activities

Physical Health

In addition to making time to maintain a healthy and balanced lifestyle, you also need to integrate daily safeguards for protecting your physical health. Keep an extra sweater and a comfortable pair of shoes in your classroom to help keep you comfortable. In addition, because stress affects your immune system, you can become more susceptible to illness. You are exposed to many illnesses brought to school by children. Illnesses spread quickly when a group of people is confined to a small area for a long period of time. Eating well, getting enough rest, drinking lots of water, frequently washing your hands with soap, and using instant hand disinfectant are just some precautions you can take to prevent colds and many of the more common illnesses.

A True Story Most teachers get sick often during the first few years of teaching. This happens because they have not yet built up their immunity against many common illnesses. I was no exception. In my first year of teaching I caught many colds and got strep throat—the first time in my life! Although teaching is a very demanding job and it is difficult to be absent, I learned the hard way that it was better to take a sick day when I was not feeling well. Pushing myself to go to work only prolonged my illnesses, and it probably made some of my students sick, too. As a result, I make sure my substitute teacher plans are always in place so that I can take a couple of sick days without having to pull together a few days of plans at the last minute.

Kidney and bladder infections are another problem for some teachers. This often results from not having enough time to use the restroom during the school day—a common teaching dilemma. Make the time! If you need to, buddy with another teacher and take turns watching each other's class so each of you can get the bathroom break you need.

You also need to be aware of procedures related to your health insurance benefits, such as taking sick days and coming in late or leaving early due to an unforeseen illness. In addition, if you should be the victim of an accident on the job, you need to know your rights and the procedures that ensure those rights.

1.2 Are there any childhood illnesses or other illnesses that you can get during the school year?

    a. Are there any vaccines available for these illnesses? Where can you get the vaccines? Who pays for them?

    b. What precautions can you take to avoid getting these illnesses?

1.3 Do you get any "sick days," "mental health days," "personal days," or "leave" days?

    a. How many do you get?

    b. What is the procedure for taking these days?

    c. Are these paid or unpaid days of absence?

1.4 What is the procedure for coming in late? leaving early? Is there a penalty for doing this?

1.5 If you get hurt on the job or elsewhere:

    a. are you required to report it? What is the procedure?

    b. what are your rights in connection with related absences, sick pay, and keeping your position? What are the procedures for receiving these benefits?

Personal Safety

In addition to illnesses, every year more and more teachers have to concern themselves with personal safety. According to the U.S. Department of Education, teachers were the victims of 1,581,000 nonfatal crimes at school, including 962,000 thefts and 619,000 violent crimes (such as rape or sexual assault, robbery, aggravated assault, and simple assault) over the 5-year period from 1992 to 1996. Among the violent crimes, 89,000 constituted serious violent crimes (such as rape or sexual assault, robbery, and aggravated assault). This translates into approximately 18,000 serious violent crimes per year. This is alarming! Every threat made against you, by a student or parent, must be taken seriously. Report it to your administration immediately. Take the measures listed below to help prevent potentially life threatening situations.

- Lock your classroom doors and windows when working alone.

- Make sure you have something in your classroom, such as a telephone, that allows you to contact the office immediately in case of an emergency.

- If anyone threatens you in any way, ask to keep your classroom doors locked during the school day until the situation is resolved.

- If your school has a policy requiring all personnel and visitors to wear identification badges, wear yours and question anyone you see who is not wearing one. Refer them to the main office to get one, and if they try to ignore your request, escort them to the office yourself or report them immediately.

- Know your classroom's neighbors, and share a code you could bang on your walls if any of you need help.

- Do not stay by yourself in your classroom after most people have gone home, especially after dark and on weekends.

- Close and lock your classroom doors before leaving in the evening.

- If you have an evening conference, ask another adult to stay with you. Also, meet the parents in a well lit common area of the building, and walk back to your cars together.

A True Story I once scheduled a parent conference very late in the evening. I was the only person left in the school building, and it felt really creepy. As a result, I waited for the parents in the school lobby and conducted our conference in the main office. Before leaving, I turned on the building's alarm system and then walked to the parking lot with the parents. Luckily, nothing bad happened. However, because I felt so uncomfortable that evening, I have never scheduled such a late conference again.

- If you have to return to school in the evening, park in a well lit area as close to the door as possible.

- Always walk with another adult to your car in the parking lot, especially after sunset.

- Be on friendly terms with your custodian, and let him know when you work after school so he can stop by to check on you.

- If your life is in danger, do not hesitate to contact the police.

If you choose to keep your classroom doors locked, make sure you are not violating any fire codes and you and your students could still vacate the room quickly in case of a fire or other emergency. By taking the measures listed above, you are taking measures to control your situation and are helping to prevent the stress associated with this unfortunate risk of the teaching profession.

1.6   What precautions can you take to help insure your physical safety from assaults and other types of abuse or personal violations?

Substances

Another health topic that comes up over and over again in the research is the use of alcohol, tobacco, and other drugs to handle stress. These substances have been found to actually do more harm than good. These substances do not alleviate stress; they just temporarily mask it. Although the stress is masked temporarily, the stressors are still there. Understand that stress prevention is the place to put your time, energy, and resources—not into a drink or a cigarette. To help eliminate the dependency of using these substances to alleviate stress, answer the following questions.

1.7   If you use alcohol, tobacco, or other drugs to alleviate stress, then

        a.   where can you find help to stop this behavior?

        b.   where can you and should you focus the time, energy, and resources that you used to spend on these substances?

Mental Health

In addition to physical health, good mental health is important for preventing stress. Mental health involves exercising the mind and keeping it fit. To accomplish this, find something that interests you that is not work related, like gardening or sports. These activities also help take your mind's focus away from stressful situations. Schedule the time to pursue these outside interests.

1.8   In which kinds of non-work related activities are you interested?

1.9   Which ones will you do? How often? Where? With whom?

Emotional Health

Emotional health is crucial for helping you prevent stress. It is very important because your beliefs about yourself and about your relationship with others impacts your self-esteem. A healthy self-esteem usually makes you better at relating to others and better at understanding your students' needs. As a result, if your stress is mostly due to how you feel about yourself or how you feel about your relationships with others, it is imperative that you take care of your emotional health.

Negative Thoughts

Controlling your negative thoughts, especially those about yourself, is one way to improve your emotional health. Three ways to control negative thoughts include replacing them, changing them, and changing your focus.

Whenever a negative thought about yourself or about your teaching enters your mind, interrupt it and replace it with a positive thought. Replace it with thoughts about past successes in your teaching career, and remember the reasons why you became a teacher in the first place.

Another way to your control negative thoughts is to change them into empowering ones. For example, instead of thinking that you will never get through grading your stack of papers, say to yourself that you will do as much as possible in the time you have allocated. If you get done, great. If you do not, then you will finish at another time. Remember to remind yourself that you are expected to do a lot more than what is often humanly possible. Therefore, you need to be realistic about what you can accomplish.

A True Story I begin every school year with fervor. I have tons of energy and lots of ideas that I add to my "to-do" list. By the third week of school, I am swamped. My list is filled with things I *have* to do in addition to all of the things I want to do. However, the differences among the items on my list get blurred, and I put a lot of pressure on myself to accomplish all of them. As a result, negative thoughts about myself run rampant. At this point, I know that I have lost sight of what *can* be done. When this happens, I step back and look at my list again. I prioritize the items and try to be realistic about what I can accomplish within the timeframe I have been given.

Changing your focus also helps remove negative thoughts. An easy way to accomplish this is by changing your activity. For example, when you are having a negative thought, change your focus by reading a good professional resource or by rearranging your bulletin boards. Keep a list of these activities taped to the inside back cover of your plan book so that the ideas are handy when you need them.

Sometimes you might also find yourself in the presence of a negative colleague. If this person's negative attitude begins to influence your thoughts, politely remove yourself from the situation. Removing yourself might help to change your focus, and thus, your negative thoughts.

Good emotional health has a lot to do with your thoughts about yourself. You need to stop beating yourself up! Every time a negative thought crosses your mind, you must interrupt it. Remember, you have complete control over what you are thinking. It is imperative that you change how you think and what you focus on in order to prevent stress.

1.10 Do you have any pervasive negative thoughts about yourself or about your teaching?

    a. What work related success have you had which can be used to replace your negative thoughts?

    b. How can you change the negative thoughts into empowering ones?

    c. What kinds of activities can you do to change your focus, especially when you are teaching?

Affirmations

You can also use affirmations to achieve emotional health. You can create positive affirmations about yourself, both personal and professional. In order for an affirmation to be effective, you must truly believe it and repeat it to yourself with all of the positive emotion you can generate. A sample empowering affirmation might be, "I am a competent and caring professional who does not react, but responds, to stressors in my environment." Use this one, or create an empowering one of your own.

1.11 What affirmations can you create that would empower you when you thought of them?

1.12 When and how often will you say these affirmations?

Being Assertive

It has been found that teachers handle stress better when they are in a supportive environment. You might be thinking, "But how do you get this support?" At first glance, you might feel that gaining support from administrators, colleagues, parents, and others is sometimes impossible. However, by becoming assertive, your chances of enlisting the support of others increases.

Being assertive means communicating your thoughts and needs efficiently and effectively using "I statements." An example is, "I feel [   ] when you [   ] because [   ]." You might also want to add "and I want [   ]." Many times you need to use these statements when someone requests that you do something for them. Being assertive helps you say "no" to things you know you should not or cannot do. If being assertive is not easy for you, do not answer the request immediately. Ask for some time and tell the other person when you will get back to her. Next, weigh the request against the things you have on your plate, as well as against your values. Then decide your response and be willing to explain how you arrived at your decision.

Being assertive is one of the ways to exercise control over the one thing you have complete control of—yourself. Take full advantage of this fact for helping you prevent stress. There are several books that can teach you how to become more assertive. If you would like more help, check out your community's and local colleges' continuing education programs for affordable classes.

1.13 Where can you learn more about becoming assertive?

1.14 How can you ensure enough time will be set aside to learn and to practice this skill?

A Support System

It is also important to identify who and where you can turn to for help and support in your times of emotional strife. Make sure that those who you identify are people you can trust. Sometimes the person who you thought you could trust stabs you in the back. Be careful! If you do not have a colleague or administrator that you can trust, confide in a spouse, a friend, or a pet. A retired teacher-friend is also a great person to talk with because they have walked in your shoes. As a result, they might be able to offer some good ideas, materials, and advice.

As part of their benefits package, employers sometimes contract with outside agencies to provide free counseling for its employees on an as needed basis. Check with your human resources department to find out if you have this service available to you. Your school's guidance department might also have this information.

If no one is available when you feel like you are going to explode, write in a journal. Get it all out on paper. Although verbal feedback from a journal is impossible, most people get a sense of relief from writing it all down because it provides an outlet for venting emotions and sorting out events. It gives a you a non-threatening environment to be very honest about a situation and about the role you played in making it a stressor. Many times, just by being able to sort out events, you find the clues for overcoming and preventing similar stressors from occurring in the future.

A True Story I began writing in a journal the first evening of my first day of student teaching. I got hooked and have kept a journal ever since. I found that it helps me vent my frustrations. It also helps me sort out the events of my life, school and non-school related. For me, my journal writing has been therapeutic. As a bonus, I also get to look back at old entries to see how much I have changed, how much I have grown. That always gives my self-esteem a boost.

1.15 Whom can you trust when you need emotional support?

1.16 If they are not available, what options do you have for getting the support you need?

Details of Your Employment

The details of your employment includes all of the paperwork required by your employer for your personnel file. There are many potential stressors in this area. Luckily, teachers have a lot of control over most of them. This part of *Step 1* analyzes the terms of your employment to help you determine exactly how much control you have over each one.

Before You Are Hired

First, briefly examine the things that an employer might require you to have before you are even hired.

1.17 What do you need to be employed by this particular school? Do they include:

    a. a background check?

        i. What kind?

        ii. Who pays for it?

        iii. What forms need to be completed?

    b. completing a formal application with the employer?

    c. proof of past work experience? What kind of proof?

    d. a teaching certification? What type of certification?

1.18 Who do you contact to find out

    a. if they received all of the above?

    b. if there are any additional items to the list above?

Your Contract

Once you have secured a job, read your contract. You must read the fine print. Read any and all paperwork, booklets, and forms associated with your employment that are mailed to you from your school system's central office. This is where many teachers actually abdicate their control without consciously being aware of it. When they do this, they are setting themselves up for turning simple, easy to handle situations into stressful experiences. Don't do this to yourself! Many of the answers to the following questions can be obtained during your interview. However, do not take anything for granted. Verify the answers with your central office and with the paperwork you receive.

1.19 What are the terms of your contract?

    a. What is the difference between a "continuing," "terminating," or other type of contract? What type of contract did you receive?

    b. Is tenure an option? How does a person earn it? How can a person lose it?

    c. What are your responsibilities and duties as stated in your contract and in your job description?

    d. Are in-service classes or other types of courses required in order to keep your

        i. job?

        ii. certification?

e. Are you required to sign up for extra duties, committees, chaperoning, detention, coaching, and others?

    i. Which ones and how many?

    ii. What are the commitments and responsibilities of each?

    iii. Do you receive a stipend for them?

f. What is the schedule for standing meetings that you are required to attend for your

    i. grade level or department?

    ii. school?

    iii. school system?

g. Are you required to attend meetings (such as faculty, PTA, workshops, and seminars) outside of school hours and during your personal time? Are you compensated for your time with money or with extra time off?

Your Class Roster

An issue that tends to cause teachers undue stress that might or might not be included in your contract is being assigned a greater than average number of students with major behavior problems. If you are a special education teacher assigned to teach this type of population, then this stressor might not apply to you. This appears to be a bigger issue for "regular education" teachers at all grade levels.

To prevent this from happening, first find out from your colleagues, administration, and office staff the school's average number of difficult students per class. Second, check your students' cumulative records as soon as you have your class roster. If you feel that you have received an unfair load, discuss it with your principal as soon as possible.

1.20 In your school, what is an average number of students per class who have significant behavior problems?

1.21 After checking your students' cumulative records, do you find you have a larger number of these kinds of students in your class? When can you speak with the principal regarding your concern?

Health Insurance Benefits

Most teaching positions also have a health insurance benefits package. Especially with the advent of health maintenance organizations (HMOs), completing the proper forms and following the correct timelines and procedures is imperative for preventing stress. The time, energy, and money lost by not following proper filing procedures can be enormous. Make sure you understand your benefits and how to get access to them.

1.22 Your health insurance benefits:

a. Who do you need to contact to find out if you have received all of the proper filing documents for obtaining or maintaining any health insurance benefits you might be entitled to?

b. Have you correctly completed and handed in all of the proper documents to obtain or maintain any health insurance benefits that you would like to receive?

c. Does the benefits enrollment office have your information recorded correctly?

d. When you visit a doctor, what are the proper filing procedures for receiving your health insurance benefits?

Financial Benefits

In addition to health insurance benefits, you also have financial benefits. Additional forms need to be completed in order to get the proper salary and the proper amount of taxes withheld from your paycheck. If this is not taken care of, you will most likely experience a lot of stress. Make sure you follow up on this area in particular.

1.23 Your financial benefits:

a. Who do you need to contact to find out if you have received all of the proper tax withholding, retirement, beneficiary, investment (such as 401K or 403B), direct deposit, and other financially-related documents that you are required to complete and have the option to complete? Where do you send them after you complete them?

b. In order to obtain the pay rate that you are entitled to, what kind of proof of past work experience, degrees, and certifications is required? Which department or person has to see this proof?

c. Is the information on your first paystub correct?

A True Story When I began teaching, I was so excited to have a job that I completely ignored all of the information on my paystub. After a few months, I began to settle into my new job and I finally took the time to look at my paystub—to really look at it. I did the math and realized there was a discrepancy between what I thought I was supposed to be paid and what I was actually being paid. I called our payroll department and inquired about the discrepancy. It turned out that my certification level was recorded incorrectly because the state had not yet notified them of my graduate degree certification status. It took a few more months to get my back pay, but I always wondered if I would have received the money if I had not brought it to their attention.

Performance Evaluations

Maintaining acceptable performance evaluations is usually a condition of employment listed in your contract. Evaluations can cause teachers a tremendous amount of stress. Stress can be minimized by finding out the exact evaluation procedures and the criteria that is used for the evaluation. Doing this decreases the number of potential misunderstandings between you and your evaluator.

You should also get to know your evaluator. Schedule a pre-evaluation meeting and glean from the conversation your evaluator's priorities. Find out which teaching styles and teacher attributes she approves of and endorses. To improve your chances of a positive evaluation, develop these styles and attributes, especially those that support your teaching philosophy, if you do not already possess them.

If you should receive a poor evaluation, you must also understand the process that follows and your rights as an employee. Find out before such an event occurs. This helps to prevent any further stress that you might have as a result of such a negative situation.

1.24 Your performance evaluations:

    a. What is the evaluation criteria?

    b. How many evaluations are required?

    c. When are they done?

    d. How is the evaluation conducted?

    e. Who formally evaluates you?

        i. When can you schedule a pre-evaluation consultation with this person?

        ii. What aspect of the teaching process is most important to her?

        iii. Which teacher does she believe is an excellent teacher? What attributes or teaching style does this person have? Which should you focus on developing and emulating to help obtain a positive evaluation at your school?

    f. When can you schedule a time to audiotape and videotape one of your lessons for critiquing your own teaching? Whose audio and video equipment can you use?

1.25 What happens if you receive a good evaluation?

1.26 What happens if you receive a poor evaluation? What are your rights as an employee?

Remember to make copies of all of your evaluations and keep them in a safe place for future reference. You might need them to help update your resume, or you might need them to support you if your teaching practices are ever questioned. Because you do not know when or why you will need to refer to them, keep copies of your evaluations and keep them safe.

A Professional Portfolio

A professional portfolio can be a valuable tool. Many professionals have portfolios. Architects, engineers, artists, and many others have portfolios that highlight their accomplishments. Teachers have known for years the power of portfolios in presenting student achievement. Likewise, you can use a professional portfolio for demonstrating your achievements as well. It can be used to demonstrate your achievements to students, to parents, to administrators, and to potential employers. You can be creative as to what a portfolio can contain, but some standard pieces should be included. They include certification certificates, transcripts, a statement of philosophy, sample unit plans and lesson plans, photographs of students working, and photographs of bulletin boards.

A True Story Every year I take pictures of all my students doing different activities. I keep them in a photo album with all of the previous years' photos. Near the end of the year I bring the photo album to school to share with my students. Many of them are interested in seeing what I have done in the past (especially if they recognize older students in the photos), and they love seeing pictures of themselves!

Whether or not you create a professional portfolio, reference letters and a reference list are good things to have in case someone requests them. Remember, discuss with your references ahead of time what they would say about you if they were ever asked. Many times your references just ask you to tell them what you would like them to say. Make sure you know what they will say before you use them as a reference!

1.27 Do you want or need to build a professional portfolio?

    a. What should it contain?

    b. Which pieces do you want to obtain this school year?

1.28 Do you need references?

    a. Who can you ask to write a reference letter on your behalf to keep in your personal career portfolio?

    b. Who can you ask to be on your list of references?

Personal and Professional Growth

Insufficient opportunities for personal and professional growth is a common concern among teachers. Teachers understand that learning does not end with the receipt of a diploma. Learning more skills, both work and non-work related, must continue for professional and personal growth. Teachers also understand that learning occurs in many different places and in many ways, not just in classrooms. This section helps you find different opportunities for continuing your education, both inside and outside of a classroom.

Professional and Educational Development Plans

Some school systems require its teachers to have some sort of professional development plan which outlines areas for further investigation and learning by the teacher. If one is not required, you might consider creating one for yourself anyway. It can be used as a guide for continuing your growth as a teacher and as a person.

1.29 Are you required to have a professional development plan?

    a. What information is required to be in the plan?

    b. Is there a form to complete?

    c. Who has to sign it?

    d. Who gets it after it is complete?

    e. How often is it reviewed?

    f. What is the procedure to update it?

Professional development plans usually include the additional education courses required by your employer. In addition to any required courses, is there anything else that you would like to learn about, career or non-career related? Whether or not they are written on an official professional development plan, make time to pursue your interests.

1.30 Are any additional courses or education required by your employer, such as

    a. in-service classes?

    b. certification renewal credits?

    c. classes towards a graduate (masters or doctorate) degree?

1.31 If additional education is not required, do you still want to take some career related courses or to do your own investigative learning about something related to your job, such as improving your classroom management skills?

1.32 Is tuition assistance available? How do you apply for it?

1.33 Do you want to learn about something that is not work related? What is it?

1.34 How can you arrange your schedule to accommodate the time needed for any of this learning and any out of class assignments that might result?

1.35 How will you evaluate whether this education has helped you?

1.36 How often will you update your educational plans?

Networking

Becoming actively involved in the profession also provides for both personal and professional growth. By joining teacher organizations, you have the opportunity to network with other teachers and to fill your calendar with social activities that support your career goals.

1.37 What local, state, and national unions and associations exist for

   a. teachers, in general?

   b. teachers in your particular field (subject, grade level, and so forth)?

1.38 How do you become a member?

Networking provides the opportunity to learn from other teachers. You can learn from other teachers by watching them, listening to them, and sharing with them. You can find these teachers in the organizations you identified above, but don't overlook the teacher next door! Your colleagues in your school and school system are treasures. They are invaluable in helping you grow, both personally and professionally. Therefore, do not isolate yourself from your colleagues.

One kind of special teacher that can have a tremendous role in helping you prevent stress is a mentor teacher. Since he usually works closely with you, he can help you identify and deal with many of the potential stressors you might face in your teaching assignment.

Master (excellent) teachers that you meet in your school are also angels sent from heaven. You can learn so much from these wonderful teachers! Most of these people have their potential stressors under control. Watch and learn from them. Do not underestimate the value of this kind of learning. It is imperative that you find these people and develop and nurture relationships with them. Use as many of your planning periods as possible to observe them. You might want to schedule a time to observe them teaching a lesson that you will also be doing to learn additional teaching strategies, or you might want to observer them teaching a lesson that you have already done in order to make comparisons.

Your relationships do not need to be one sided—give as well as receive. For example, for those who have helped you, offer to watch their classes during your free periods or write a sincere note of appreciation and copy your principal.

1.39 Will you be assigned a mentor?

   a. Who is he?

   b. What is the relationship between mentor and mentee?

   c. In what ways can he help you?

   d. What are your responsibilities to him?

1.40 Who are the master teachers in your school and in your school system?

   a. What kinds of things can you learn from them?

   b. What kinds of things do you want to learn from them?

c. How can you learn from them?

d. Can you schedule a time to meet and observe these teachers?

e. May you ask one of them to be your mentor?

1.41 What kinds of things can you do to show your appreciation for these special people?

Giving and Receiving

When you give your time and resources to other teachers, you receive much more in return. By helping your colleagues solve their stress related problems, you can gain insight into your own stress and actually decrease the amount of stress you are feeling. By supporting one another, you can reduce feelings of isolation and helplessness and become more emotionally and socially healthy individuals. If an entire group of teachers supports one another, the teaching team becomes more effective. Therefore, you need to examine ways in which you can work together with other teachers to prevent and deal with stress.

Peer Coaching

Peer coaching is one way to give and to receive help. In peer coaching, two or more teachers with mutual trust and rapport agree to observe and to coach one another. They focus on helping one another sharpen specific teaching strategies and skills, ones they feel they need to improve.

The teachers agree to meet before and after a peer observation. They meet before the observation to decide which teacher behaviors (strategies and skills) are observed and what instruments are used to collect the data. After the observation, they have a post conference to give specific feedback. Being as objective as possible, they discuss how the specific strategy or skill is being implemented. They also discuss ways to improve the strategy or skill and schedule a follow up observation. Because teachers are not attacking one another, peer coaching is a non-threatening way to get support.

Another way to implement peer coaching is to create a team of teachers that agree to present model lessons for one another. In this way, no one is critiquing anyone else and everyone is learning from each other.

1.42 Is peer coaching something that you are interested in pursuing? Which teachers do you feel you can help and who will give you the most honest feedback in a supportive manner?

Peer Support Groups

Another way of working together to prevent stress is establishing peer support groups. The purpose of these support groups is to help one another clarify stress-related problems and to brainstorm solutions. Effective support groups have a deep level of trust and rapport. They also start and stop on time. They have a set agenda and stick to it. The procedure for these support group meetings and their accompanying challenge sheet can be found in appendix A.

Like a journal, peer support groups give a teacher a non-threatening environment in which to be honest and objective about a stressor. An additional benefit of having established peer support groups is knowing you have a group of people you can trust when you need help.

1.43   Have peer support groups already been established in your school or school system? If yes, how does a teacher join one? If no, can you start one? What will you need to establish a group?

Sharing Information

As a teacher, you are bombarded with information. A lot of this information might not be useful to you but might be useful to someone else. Pass the information along. It might help someone else solve a problem and prevent stress. In addition, when we help others deal with their stress, our own stress level decreases. Therefore, it is very important that we never lose sight of the fact that in giving, we receive.

1.44   In what ways can you help other teachers?

   a.   What kinds of things can you share with them?

   b.   If you attend a workshop or seminar, how can you share with your colleagues what you have learned?

   c.   What vehicles can you use to share information with other teachers in your grade level or department, school, school system, state, country, and world?

A True Story We are sometimes forced to work with colleagues who appear to be very territorial with their materials and ideas. Whether it is because they feel threatened by other teachers, they do not respect their peers' teaching styles and expertise, or they get so caught up in their own class that they cannot see what else is going on around them, colleagues who do not share perpetuate the "sink or swim" situation in which many teachers often find themselves. As mentioned earlier, teaching can be a very lonely job, especially if you are surrounded by colleagues who do not share their ideas and materials. Unfortunately, I have experienced this more than once. All teachers, experienced and new, have something to offer. If we take the time and effort to share with one another, we all will be more successful. Just imagine!

Summary

Taking care of yourself includes taking care of both your personal and your professional needs. In addition to taking control of your life, it is important to help others gain control of their lives, too. Our stress decreases when we help others.

This step is the most important of all seven steps. It shows us how to take control over the only thing we can completely control—ourselves. *Step 1: Take Care of Yourself*, is the footings upon which the rest of the foundation is built. The rest of the foundation is made up of *Step 2: Understand the Expectations* and *Step 3: Know Your Resources*.

Chapter 3

Step 2:

Understand the Expectations

Understanding the expectations that are placed upon you as a teacher plays a significant role in helping you prevent stress. For example, when your expectations about your role as a teacher are different than your employer's expectations, you can be sure that there will be tension. This tension is a stressor for you and for everyone else involved. If you learn about and understand your employer's expectations before the possibility of a confrontation, you have more control over the situation. You have choices. The choices are either to meet the expectations or to take an assertive approach to try to resolve your differences amicably.

There are two kinds of stressors related to expectations. They are role conflict and role ambiguity.

When you are pulled in different directions by parents, students, administrators, and colleagues, you experience role conflict. In role conflict, you get conflicting demands about what you are supposed to do. For example, you might be encouraged by your central office administration to use cooperative learning centers, yet school administrators expect you to operate a teacher-centered classroom where your students are to work quietly by themselves. The conflicting messages about which teaching style you should use can cause stress.

Role ambiguity, on the other hand, is not knowing the exact expectations and goals of the job. For example, if you are not given a curriculum guide, course of study, or some other kind of outline for the subject or grade level you are teaching, you might not be sure what you are supposed to teach. Also, if you are not given the criteria which is used by your school for teacher evaluations, you will not know how you will be judged. As a result, you will experience role ambiguity and the stress that comes with it.

In order to prevent role conflict and role ambiguity, identify and understand your own expectations first. Second, identify and understand the expectations of all the people you interface with.

Learn as much as you can about others' expectations *before* you start your teaching assignment. However, it is inevitable that after you start the assignment, several things will come up on a daily basis that challenge your expectations of your job and of your role as a teacher. Be prepared! Try to understand as much as you can before your first day so that you are better prepared. Be assertive and resolve any mismatches in expectations before they become issues for either you or the other person.

Identify Your Expectations

The first step for preventing role conflict and role ambiguity is to identify your own expectations. However, before you write them in concrete, realize and accept the fact that your expectations will change over time. They change because you change. You change as a result of the growth you experience from being faced with new challenges day after day, year after year. If you understand this up front, it might help you be more flexible and less frustrated when your current expectations are challenged by your new knowledge and experience.

> **A True Story** As a new teacher, I was very idealistic. My expectations about myself, my students, and my job were unrealistic. I know that many new teachers, independent of their age or of their assignment, have a similar experience. Perhaps it is due to a romantic notion of how we believe teaching should be. Perhaps it is due to the excitement of a new job, a fresh start, a clean slate. Or perhaps it is the conviction that we will make a difference in the lives of our students regardless of what is happening in all of our lives outside of school. I don't know. What I do know, however, is that over time, I changed. I grew as a result of my experiences, both positive and negative, and my expectations changed accordingly. To be realistic, I also expect them to keep changing as I continue to grow.

In addition, it is important to know the research about effective teaching as you formulate your current expectations. The research might shape your own expectations about your role as a teacher. Remember, effective teachers are more in control of their classes, of their careers, and of their lives. Having this control goes a long way in helping prevent stress.

The Effective Teacher

There is a lot of research related to instruction and expectations. The research shows that teachers who have the highest student achievement usually have the following attributes:

- have a belief that students can and will learn
- put emphasis on academic goals and activities
- set high but attainable goals for academic performance

It has been found that teachers are more successful if they do the following:

- explain the educational objectives of the lesson
- use direct instruction with lower achieving and younger students
- supervise students' work
- give feedback

It is interesting to note it has been found that giving feedback is the teacher behavior that matters most for strong student achievement.

The research also shows that when it comes to discipline, the effective teacher does the following:

- punishes less
- is more supportive and reassuring
- uses a positive reward system
- reprimands softly and only when necessary
- allows the offender to save face

It also has been found that teachers who monitor student behavior not only have more contact with students during seatwork, they also quickly attend to students' inappropriate behavior to help prevent discipline problems (one of the leading stressors associated with teaching). Therefore, it is worthwhile for you to be "with-it," to be aware of your students' behavior at all times.

In addition to the findings above, do not forget to do your own research. Look around you and find which teachers in your school are most effective. They are usually the ones who are highly respected by administrators, students, and parents. Figure out why. If the attributes and attitudes that make them successful are congruent with your beliefs and values, emulate them. Also, use the same teaching strategies, set up your classroom in a similar way, and follow a similar routine. Copy the things they do that you feel would be most beneficial in helping you, too, become an effective teacher.

2.1 Which teachers are effective?

a. Why?

b. What are their expectations about teaching? administrators? students? parents?

c. Which attributes and attitudes would be helpful to emulate?

d. Which things that they do would be helpful to copy?

Your Teaching Philosophy

In light of all of the above research findings, what are your beliefs about effective teaching?

2.2   What is your philosophy about

    a.   learning?

    b.   homework and parents' role in homework?

    c.   assessing and evaluating learning?

    d.   effective instructional strategies for your students?

    e.   discipline and the roles you, parents, and administrators play as disciplinarians?

    f.   reward systems for

        i.   behavior?

        ii.   academic achievement?

Your Expectations

Using your philosophy about effective teaching as a base, what do you expect from this teaching experience? What are your expectations of others? Use the following additional questions to help you sort it out.

2.3   What are your expectations about your job?

    a.   What teaching assignments and classes are you expecting to get? How many students?

    b.   With what kinds of student needs do you expect to be faced? How do you expect your students to be in terms of behavior, motivation, values, and beliefs?

    c.   What do you think your job will be like?

    d.   How much support do you expect to receive from administrators? colleagues? students? parents?

A True Story I began my elementary school teaching career in a newly built school. Because the school had no history, every procedure and rule had to be created. Every detail of opening a new school had to be attended to. This left very little time and energy to support the handful of first year teachers like myself. As a result, I recommend that first year teachers look very closely at the school in which they will be working. Investigate how much collegial support you can expect to receive because you will need lots of it as a first year teacher. Do not underestimate this.

---

    e.   How do you expect to be addressed by your students? students' parents? colleagues and administrators?

Now that you have identified your expectations, it is important for you to identify what others expect of you.

Identify Federal and State Expectations

Although many of the expectations at the federal and state level are not made of you on a personal level, in the United States you are involved in a profession that must comply to certain laws and government regulations, such as the Individuals with Disabilities Education Act (IDEA). As a result, you must do your part to help your school be in compliance with these laws and regulations.

There are several laws of which you must be aware because violating these laws opens the door for lawsuits against your school system, your school, and you. Prevent this from happening. Learn about the laws that affect you and your students from your school system's Special Education Department. Your state's department of education and the federal government's department of education are also good sources. Know the law, and understand how it is interpreted.

2.4   What federal and state education laws affect your school?

2.5   With what other laws or regulations (for example, Occupational Safety and Health Administration (OSHA) and child abuse and neglect reporting laws) must your school be in compliance?

> **A True Story** Many teachers reviewed this book before it was printed. It is interesting to note that although none of the newer teachers made any notes in this section, most of the teachers with twenty or more years of experience wrote a comment in this section that restated its importance.

Identify the Community's Expectations

The community is the predominant force in defining the expectations of your school. Therefore, it is important that you get to know the community which your school and school system serve. Subscribe to the local paper. Visit the community and shop at local establishments. Call or visit the local Chamber of Commerce and the area's visitor's center. Get to know the social and emotional climate of the community. It tells you a lot about what you can expect as a teacher in their schools.

What the community expects from your school becomes reflected in your school system's mission statement. The community's expectations of its schools and the laws with which the school system must comply are funneled together to create a mission statement for the school system. Sometimes additional ones are created for each individual school. Understanding these mission statements and how they are achieved give you a general understanding of your role as an educator in this particular school system.

    2.6   What are the mission statements of your:

        a.   school system?

        b.   school?

    2.7   How are these missions achieved by the

        a.   school system?

        b.   school?

School System Policies

Mission statements might tell you what a school system believes it is supposed to do. School system policies show you how they intend to do it. School system policies, which are sometimes further embellished at the school, grade, or department level, are highly reflective of the expectations of the community it serves. Staff, parent, and student handbooks are good sources for this information. If they exist, read them.

    2.8   Where can you obtain a copy of the following handbooks (if they exist)?

        a.   staff

        b.   student

        c.   parent

    2.9   What are your school system's, school's, grade's, and department's policies, written *and* unwritten, for students *and* staff (when applicable) regarding

        a.   discipline (including assaulting, fighting, stealing, sexual harassment, weapons, gangs, drugs, alcohol, profanity, and so forth)? Are there any specific procedures or forms to be completed when involving administrators in discipline related matters, such as sending a student to the office or to detention?

        b.   appearance (including dress code)?

        c.   homework?

        d.   instruction, including acceptable teaching styles and teaching strategies?

Rights and Freedoms

In addition to federal and state education laws and local policies, you must also be aware of the United States Constitution's Bill of Rights and how your community supports it. Although these rights are protected by the government, you still need to find out the boundaries your school system places on these rights. The boundaries reflect the values and expectations of the community it serves. Understand them to help you understand your role in meeting the expectations of your community.

2.10 What boundaries, if any, are placed on the rights of freedom of speech, of the press, of assembling peaceably, and of petitioning? How do these boundaries affect you and your role as a teacher?

Along these same lines, does your school or school system limit the use of certain materials or discourage certain topics from being explored and discussed? Find out the following:

2.11 Are there any books or resources whose use is discouraged or even prohibited by your school or school system?

2.12 Are there any topics or themes whose discussion is discouraged or even prohibited by your school or school system?

Curriculum

In continuing to find out what you are not supposed to discuss, it is also very important to find out what you *must* discuss. This is usually documented in a curriculum guide or standard course of study. In addition to the subject matter to be taught, sometimes this information also includes what materials, instructional strategies, and classroom climate you are expected to use to meet the curriculum goals.

2.13 What is the curriculum or standard course of study for the classes you teach?

2.14 What materials and instructional strategies are you expected to use?

2.15 What kind of classroom climate is expected?

A True Story As an instructional resource teacher whose primary job is to share curriculum with teachers, I have really embraced the value of a documented curriculum. A documented curriculum prevents gaps in students' knowledge and skills. It also prevents "curriculum overlap" which can cause student boredom (and therefore, discipline problems). However, many problems arise when teachers do not follow the curriculum. For example, I once did an activity where some of my students exclaimed, "We did this last year!" As a result, some of my students tuned out the lesson and did not learn as much as they could have. The situation also invited discipline problems and increased my frustration level. If we, the teachers in my school, had been following the curriculum, there would have been a much higher probability that we would not have had an overlap. Therefore, make sure you are reading your curriculum guides and teaching what you are supposed to be teaching. It will keep you out of trouble with your students, administration, and parents.

Programs for Exceptional Students

Because children function at very different developmental levels regardless of their grade level or placement, curriculum goals and objectives might need to be modified to meet students' needs. Although there are laws protecting the exceptional student, especially those who are low achieving and have been found to have a type of physical, psychological, or emotional disability, the local community might demand more from its school system for meeting the needs of these students.

How much the curriculum is modified or enhanced above and beyond what the law would normally provide for these children is very reflective of the values and beliefs of vocal people in the community. These people might push for a more individualized and a more challenging curriculum for high achieving students, sometimes labeled "academically gifted" students. They might also push for additional special services on an Individual Education Plan (IEP) for a child with physical and psychological needs. Therefore, you need to know if there are any extra programs and services that the school system or school has set up to meet the additional demands of the community.

2.16 How does your school system and school meet the needs of the following exceptional children?

    a. above average academic achievers

    b. musically, artistically, and athletically gifted

    c. below average academic achievers

    d. children with physical, psychological, or emotional disabilities

School Rules and Procedures

In addition to programs for exceptional students, there are also school rules and procedures that affect all students. These rules and procedures also affect staff and parents. They have been put in place to help the school system and school run smoothly, and must be followed. Find out about them by asking the following questions.

2.17 What are the rules and procedures for students and staff regarding:

    a. arrival at school (inside and outside the school building)?

    b. early morning programs (for those who arrive for morning on-site daycare or other programs)?

    c. dismissal (inside and outside the school building)?

    d. after school programs (after school daycare or other programs)?

2.18 Attendance:

    a. Where are the records kept?

    b. Who does the recording?

    c. Is it recorded in pen or pencil?

    d. What are the symbols used for recording an absence?

    e. What are considered excused and inexcused absences?

f. Is any documentation from home required when a student returns to school after being absent?

g. How is tardiness recorded?

h. Who gets the daily attendance record after it is completed and by what time?

i. What is the follow up procedure if a student is absent? Who does it?

j. What is the procedure for signing in and out during the instructional day?

k. Is the absentee list posted daily, especially for use by resource teachers and other specialists that work with students in a pull-out program (a program where the students go to another classroom for instruction) or push-in program (a program where a teacher comes into your classroom to work with a student or group of students)?

2.19 What are the school discipline rules that your class must follow and the discipline programs that your class must use?

a. Are teachers allowed to send students to the office? Under what circumstances?

b. What can students expect when they meet with a disciplinarian in the office?

2.20 What are the rules and the procedures for the use of the:

a. hallways?

    i. Are you required to escort your students in the hallways?

    ii. Are "hallway passes" required?

b. hallway lavatories?

c. cafeteria?

    i. How do students and teachers obtain lunch tickets or accounts?

    ii. Where can you obtain copies of free and reduced lunch application forms?

    iii. Do you need to take lunch count and collect lunch money in the mornings?

    iv. Are there assigned seats?

    v. Do you need to use a specific traffic pattern?

    vi. Where are trays, plates, and utensils returned and where is trash thrown out?

    vii. Are there student or teacher cleaning duties?

a. media center/library?

    i. Are "library passes" required?

    ii. How long can a student and a teacher keep a book on loan?

b. gymnasium?

c. computer room?

d. auditorium?

    e. playground areas?

    f. playground equipment?

    g. parking lots? Do students and staff get assigned parking spaces?

    h. schoolbus?

    i. common areas (inside and outside)?

2.21 Emergency procedures:

    a. What emergency procedures must your class follow during:

        i.   a fire?

        ii.   severe weather?

        iii. an injury?

        iv. an illness?

    b. Are you required to post any of the above procedures?

    c. After an accident, are you required to fill out an accident report? How much time do you have to complete it?

2.22 The school health office:

    a. How does the health office personnel support you and your class?

    b. What are the health office's rules and procedures?

    c. Which ones of your students' illnesses (for example, head lice, chicken pox, and so forth) are you required to report to the health office?

    d. What emergency contact information is collected from your students? Are you required to collect it? When? How?

    e. What is the procedure for calling parents when a student is sick and needs to go home? How do you find out who is allowed to pick up the student from school?

    f. What are the rules and procedures for administering medications to students?

        i.   What associated forms must be completed by the student's parents? physician? teachers?

        ii.   Who contacts the parent or physician when prescriptions need refilling?

        iii. Are students allowed to self-medicate?

    g. Are first aid kits available?

2.23 What is the procedure for "lost and found" items?

2.24 What are the procedures and rules regarding the use of the school's petty cash account? Do you get reimbursed for any out-of-pocket expenses? If yes, what is the procedure for getting your reimbursement?

2.25 What are the procedures and rules regarding handing in field trip money, fund-raising money, and other money which is collected from students?

    a. Who is the money given to? By what time each day must this person collect the money?

    b. Is there a form that you must complete to accompany your deposit?

A True Story I will never forget the first time I collected field trip money. I collected the money each day and kept it locked in my file cabinet. One day the school secretary asked me if I had begun collecting the field trip money. I told her I had, and she exclaimed that I was supposed to give my collections to her by noon every day. I was also required to complete and sign a special form stating how much I had given to her and when. Until that day, I never knew that teachers had to deposit on a daily basis any money they had collected from students. Luckily, my school secretary was very understanding.

2.26 What is the procedure for reserving a classroom or a conference room for meetings, staff development meetings, or other gatherings?

2.27 Which school telephones can you use for personal use and for work related use?

2.28 Are school supplies such as paper, pencils, and pens, provided for your students or are they expected to supply their own? If they are to supply their own and cannot afford them, who provides the school supplies for them?

2.29 May you request a list of school supplies, monetary contributions, or other donations from students and their families?

Many of the rules and procedures mentioned above are usually needed in the first few days and weeks of school. Have this information prepared for students and parents as soon as possible. You might want to add it to a Classroom Handbook (which will be discussed later in this chapter) and distribute it to your students and their parents on the first day of school.

Special Activities

Special activities that occur throughout the year might also have rules and procedures associated with them. Use the following questions to find out what they are.

2.30 Holidays:

    a. Which special events or holidays are you allowed to celebrate in your classes? Which ones do you want to celebrate?

    b. What can and cannot be done to celebrate holidays? (See appendix B for tips on planning celebrations.)

  c. Does anyone have to be notified of these activities? Does anyone have to sign off on these activities?

  d. What is the policy for:

    i. having religious holiday paraphernalia displayed (such as a Christmas tree, a menorah, and so forth)?

    ii. discussing religious holidays in your class?

2.31 What can and cannot be done to celebrate a student's or a colleague's birthday during school hours and on school campus?

2.32 Are there programs or events in which your grade level or department traditionally host or participate?

  a. When are they held?

  b. What is your role in organizing and participating in the events?

2.33 What is the tradition at your school regarding end of year picnics and celebrations? Is each class responsible to set up their own or are they school-wide events?

A True Story I worked at a school where some teachers held their own end of year class picnics in addition to the traditional school-wide end of year celebrations. Since I was unaware of this tradition, I was one of the few teachers that did not plan for one. My students and their parents asked me repeatedly about having a picnic, but when they began asking, it was already too late in the year to plan for one. I felt badly for my students and vowed to never let a "fun" tradition pass by me ever again!

2.34 What fund-raisers occur, if any? What is your role in these activities?

2.35 Are you expected and allowed to take class trips? (If yes, see appendix C for tips on planning class trips.)

2.36 Book fairs:

  a. Are any scheduled?

  b. If your students need assistance in choosing books, who helps them?

  c. Do any of your students qualify for any free books due to prizes or financial assistance?

  d. Are you allowed to create a "wish list" to be used by parents as a guideline when purchasing books to donate to your classroom?

2.37 Are you required to have a classroom student recognition program (such as "Student of the Week," "Show and Tell," and so forth)?

Unstated Rules and Procedures

Every school has a unique culture. For example, certain schools expect you to be involved in every faculty social activity, while other schools don't. As a result, every school has unstated rules and procedures that reflect their unique culture. Get to know what these rules are by observing and speaking with your colleagues.

2.38 What is the professional etiquette in your school? What do your colleagues expect from you professionally?

2.39 What are the unstated rules of the teachers' lounge? Who pays for the coffee and who makes it? Who get to eat the "free food" people sometimes place in the lounge?

2.40 What are the rules (stated and unstated) for borrowing materials from your school's professional library? How many items can you have on loan at one time? How long can you keep them?

A True Story For several months I could not find a professional resource in my school's professional library. Some of the other teachers kept telling me that our school had it and it was there, but I just could not find it. At the end of the school year, I found out that one of my colleagues had used it and had kept it in her classroom practically the entire school year. As a result, I felt frustrated. I learned to prevent stress by asking *all* of my colleagues about missing resources instead of just asking a few.

2.41 Are you expected to welcome unannounced classroom visits and observations by administrators? parents?

2.42 Are you expected to join the PTA?

2.43 If you witness an argument or other problem outside your classroom, are you expected to discipline students whom you do not teach? How much are you expected to do before calling other school personnel for help?

2.44 If your students are involved in intramural sports, band, music lessons, cheerleading, color guard, and other extra curricular activities,

   a. are there any special activities that occur during the school year for them? What is your role in these special activities?

   b. are you expected to allow students to leave early from class or come late to class in order to participate in any of these activities?

   c. are you expected to change or alter assignments, such as due dates, for students involved in particular extracurricular activities?

Responsibilities

Besides knowing and following rules and procedures, there are many things that you have to do as a teacher. They are your responsibilities. Most of them are documented in a staff handbook (if one exists). If one does not exist, the questions below help point out key responsibilities that most teachers have.

2.45 Paperwork (see "Possible Types of Paperwork" below for a list of paperwork that might be required):

    a.   What paperwork, if any, is required for your position?

    b.   To whom do you deliver it?

    c.   When is it due?

    d.   What is the frequency of completing this paperwork?

    e.   What format is required?

Possible Types of Paperwork

Check to see if forms already exist for some of these or if particular formats are expected.

- attendance, tardy, and absentee notices
- milk money and lunch forms
- lesson plans
- students' assignments (grading and filing)
- student progress reports for school administrators
- tests (creating and grading)
- grade book
- plan book
- report cards and other student evaluation reports
- daily or weekly homework folders
- academic and behavior contracts
- student referral forms for special services and Individualized Education Plans (IEPs)

- grade level/course retention paperwork
- weekly newsletters
- parent notes
- parent-teacher conference records (in person or via telephone calls)
- daily or weekly academic and behavior reports
- parent questionnaires and surveys
- students' cumulative/permanent records
- meeting minutes
- substitute teacher folders (creating and maintaining)
- student "self-discipline"(including effort and behavior) reports
- emergency contact cards
- end of year card summarizing student's achievement and placement for following year

---

2.46 What is your responsibility to update and maintain students' cumulative/permanent folders?

     a. What information goes in them?

     b. Where are the folders kept?

     c. What is the order of the documents placed in the folders?

2.47 Lesson Plans:

     a. Is there a lesson plan format that must be used?

     b. Are your lesson plans or plan book reviewed? How often and by whom?

     c. Are you required to leave your plan book at school?

2.48 Extra Duties:

     a. Are you assigned any extra duties, or are you expected to volunteer for them?

     b. What are the responsibilities of the different extra duties available?

2.49 Are you required to attend certain meetings? What are they, and when and where are they held?

2.50 Do you have to complete purchase orders for teaching and student materials for your classes, your grade level, your department, special classes (such as Art, Music, Media, P.E., Foreign Language, and so forth), resource classes, or other?

2.51 Are you required to stay with your students during their special classes such as Art, Music, P.E., Foreign Language, and so forth or during their lunch period?

Accountability

Accounting for student progress is one of your responsibilities. The community at large expects a lot from its schools, and consequently, a lot from you. Barry Farber describes these expectations so well. He writes, "Society expects [you] to educate, socialize, and graduate virtually every student who comes to school, regardless of the social, economic, familial, or psychological difficulties some of these students bring with them." He adds that parents, psychologists, social workers, and agencies can fail, but teachers cannot. Teachers will be held accountable. Farber believes that the push for accountability is just a way of expecting schools to cure the ills of society. Farber poses an interesting point of view. Many teachers who have experienced disgruntled parents and community members know that there is some truth to what he is saying.

The community, especially parents of school aged children, are crying for accountability. They want to know if their schools are doing their job. They want to know if children are learning. To determine these things, the community relies very heavily on test results and grades.

The system used to show accountability is usually representative of the community's expectations. However, be forewarned! Some community members, especially parents, are not satisfied with the reporting mechanisms that are currently in place. They want more information. Ask your colleagues and principal if parents are looking for additional assessment information or for the information to be presented in a different format. Furthermore, many parents find some of our reporting mechanisms unfamiliar and confusing. Sometimes using layman's terms to explain what the grades and test results mean and to compare them to an *average* student's achievement helps to clear up confusion and alleviate parent frustration and fears. Effective communication about student achievement goes a long way in helping you prevent stress.

2.52   Standardized tests:

    a.   What standardized tests are used in your school?

    b.   Which ones will your students be taking?

    c.   When and how do the test results get shared with students and parents?

    d.   What do you need to do to help prepare your students for these tests?

    e.   What do you need to do to prepare yourself for administering these tests?

2.53   Reporting student progress:

    a.   What is reported on report cards or their equivalent?

    b.   Are portfolios required? What is the minimum required contents?

    c.   How are grades determined? Do effort, participation, and homework completion get factored into the grades?

    d.   Are report cards, or their equivalent, reviewed by anyone on the staff before being shared with the students and their parents?

    e.   Are parent-teacher conferences required? When and where?

    f.   Are student "self-discipline" (including effort and behavior) daily or weekly reports expected by parents?

    g.   Are daily or weekly homework or classwork folders expected to be sent home with students?

A True Story I worked in a school that allowed each teacher to choose the day which was best for them for sending home weekly classwork folders. As a result, there was a lot of inconsistency, even among teachers at the same grade level. Mid year we received a new assistant principal, and she felt it was necessary to be consistent across all classes in the school. As a result, all of the teachers chose the same day to send home weekly folders. This common routine brought a sense of unity to our school. It also made a positive impression on parents.

Substitute Teacher Plans

You are also held accountable for your students' learning when you are absent. Because of this, put together excellent emergency substitute teacher plans. Although this responsibility is sometimes put at the bottom of the "to do list," make it a priority. Lesson plans are the last thing you want to do from your sick bed! Your mind and body will be stressed enough from your illness or accident. Having sufficient, quality substitute teacher plans in place helps you prevent stress when you need to prevent it the most.

2.54   Substitute Teacher Plans:

    a.   What must they include? If there is no guideline, what kinds of information does the substitute teacher need in order to have a successful, productive day (see appendix D for a sample list of things)?

    b.   Can the directions left be easily understood by a substitute teacher and by your students?

    c.   In order to prevent student discipline problems,

        i.   are the lessons stimulating with a high student interest level?

        ii.   do these plans keep students actively involved and on task?

        iii.   do the activities ensure a high success rate?

    d.   How many days of substitute plans are you required to have prepared?

    e.   Where are you supposed to keep them (in the classroom, in the main office, or other place)? If there is no set rule, where can you keep them so that they are easily accessible in an emergency by a substitute teacher?

    f.   How often are you required to update your emergency substitute teacher plans? If there is no requirement, how often do you feel is necessary?

Working with Parents

When building relationships with parents, communication is the key. You need to build a relationship that is based on the fact that you are two adults concerned about a student's progress. You are not best buddies, nor are you enemies.

You need to know their expectations of you to help build successful relationships. Find out what they expect from you by asking them. Send home a simple survey at the beginning of the year addressing many of the points below. Also, you might want to ask your colleagues what they believe parents want, especially the colleagues that taught your students the previous year. However, just like everyone else, people do change, and some parents might have different expectations this year. Some might even want to wipe the slate clean with the new school year. If this is the impression that you get when you meet them, respect their wishes.

2.55   What kinds of information do parents want?

2.56   What types of communication vehicles do parents expect you to use (such as letters, newsletters, telephone calls, or conferences) when communicating with them?

2.57 Is it expected that you communicate with them on a:

    a. prescribed frequency?

    b. frequency that you get to decide?

    c. as needed basis?

Please note that when calling a parent on the telephone, remember that it is courteous to first ask if it is a good time to speak with them. If not, reschedule a time that is good for both of you.

Parent-Teacher Conferences

When it comes to parent-teacher conferences, parent or teacher initiated, send a questionnaire to the parents asking them what they think are their child's strengths and weaknesses. You might also want to find out if they have any concerns about their child's progress, what their beliefs are about what they can do at home to support their child's progress, and if they have any questions. This questionnaire should be returned to you well in advance of the conference so that you can prepare yourself and your supporting materials. See appendix E for tips on conducting successful parent-teacher conferences.

Keeping it Positive

Parents expect that their school system will make them feel proud of their children and of the school system and community with which they belong. Find out how your school system and school meets this expectation and your role in accomplishing it.

2.58 What things does your school system and school do to make parents feel proud of their

    a. children?

    b. school?

    c. school system?

    d. community?

2.59 What specific programs does your school system and school have in place for student recognition?

2.60 What is your role in accomplishing these things?

2.61 What additional things can you do to further this effort?

Involving Parents

Another way to get parents (and community members) to feel proud of their school is to get them involved in positive activities. However, not everyone will, or even wants to, get involved.

You might have three types of parents represented in your class: those who are occasionally involved, those who are too involved, and those who are not involved enough. The parents who are too involved could actually become a burden to you, unless you channel their energies into classroom-enhancing activities. On the other end of the spectrum, the parents who are never involved could also be a burden to you because it might require a great deal of your time and effort just to contact them.

Regardless of the type of parents you have, you need to find out what their expectations are for involvement (a survey might be helpful), and you need to get them involved.

2.62 How do parents (working and non-working) expect to be involved in their child's school life and in their school?

2.63 What does your school system and school expect you to do to involve parents (working and non-working)? other community members?

2.64 What can you ask parents and community members to do or not to do?

A True Story There is a school that has a committee which sets up guidelines regarding parent involvement. These guidelines are included in a parent handbook to help parents, especially those who volunteer often, understand the school's expectations of their involvement. In this way, these guidelines offer documented limits for both parents and teachers.

When Parents Are Not Satisfied

One final note with respect to working with parents: when parents have concerns about their child's education, they sometimes make demands for some particular change that they feel will help correct the situation. For example, they might demand a change in the placement of their child in a particular class or course. They might also make demands about your class' curriculum and instruction.

You need to know how your principal and how your school system administrator responds to these demands and how they expect *you* to respond. Furthermore, you need to understand how parents expect you to react. Do they expect you to cave into their demands? Do they expect you to compromise? Do they expect you to refer them to someone else? If a parent has been used to having teachers and administrators cave into their demands and you do not back down, you can be sure that you will have a sticky situation on your hands. By understanding how that parent reacts and why, you can alter your response accordingly. You might be able to diffuse the situation by just remaining calm.

This type of situation can cause significant role conflict for a teacher. Beware of this major stressor, and take precautions by knowing others' expectations and being prepared with your responses ahead of time.

2.65 How does each parent expect you to respond when they make demands about a change in their child's curriculum, instruction, or placement?

2.66 How does your employer respond to parent demands?

2.67 How does your employer expect you to respond to parent demands?

Reporting Grievances

No matter what the school system and school do to meet the expectations of the community it serves, there still might be someone who is not satisfied. When this occurs, there is usually (hopefully) a policy or procedure in place for parents and for other community members to communicate a grievance and to get a response to it. Find out what this is. Refer people with grievances regarding issues outside of your control to this process. It helps them direct their energies into the proper channels. This also helps to decrease, or even remove, a stressor in your life.

2.68 What is the procedure that parents and other community members can use to communicate a grievance against you, your school, or your school system?

Identify Your Students' Expectations

In addition to all of the expectations generated by the adults in your school's local community, you need to also remember that your students also have expectations. They range from how they expect you to behave to how their educational experience should be. Before you meet your students, you can take an educated guess about what they are expecting. If and when the subject is appropriate, you might even want to ask your students directly.

2.69 How do your students expect you to dress and to behave?

2.70 What things do your students expect you to do or say to
   a. support them and their learning?
   b. help them feel proud of themselves, of their school, and of their academic and affective progress?
   c. provide them with feedback?

2.71 What do they expect are your expectations of them?

2.72 What are their expectations regarding how their progress is assessed and graded?

2.73 Do your students expect rewards for good behavior, good work, and so forth?

One last note about student expectations deals with grades. Students have some expectation of how you determine their grades. They might also have a belief that you *give* them grades, that you are the king or queen handing down rewards and punishments. Many students have not learned, for reasons relating to conditioning and associations of past experiences with grades, that their grades are *earned*. As their teacher, you must help them understand that their grades are earned, and for the most part, they are greatly determined by the amount of effort they put into their learning. If you can show them that *they* have control over their grades, the ownership of learning is transferred to your students (and rightfully so), and you prevent a potential stressor.

Sharing Your Expectations— The Classroom Handbook

Understand that expectations flow in both directions. Just as you want to learn about what others expect of you, others, especially your students and their parents, want to know what you expect of them. Although there are many ways to share your expectations, a Classroom Handbook is a great vehicle, especially for students and their parents.

The "Sample Table of Contents for a Classroom Handbook" on page 58 shows a sample table of contents for one such handbook. A good idea is to share this information with your students on the first day of school and with parents at an Open House or Back to School Night. Your principal might be interested in this information, too.

> 2.74 How can you make your expectations known to your
>
> > a. employer?
> >
> > b. colleagues?
> >
> > c. students?
> >
> > d. students' parents?

A Final Note About Expectations

Expectations are dynamic. They can and do change. Circumstances, sometimes totally beyond your control, warrant the expectations to change, even after the first day of school.

If a change in expectations forces you to alter what you are doing or what you have planned, discuss possible solutions with your colleagues and phase in the change. Be realistic. Don't try to be superhuman. You can only implement changes at a rate *you* can change.

Be careful not to think that once you have all of the above answered that you are set for the school year. Do not let this upset you! Accept the fact that your expectations change and others' expectations change, too. Keep your eyes and ears open at all time for any changes. However, until you are aware

Sample Table of Contents for a Classroom Handbook

The following are possible sections of a Classroom Handbook that you can create to help others learn about your expectations. Also consider creating your entire handbook in a FAQ (Frequently Asked Questions) format.

- your teaching and instructional philosophies
- overview of the curriculum for the school year
- how grades are determined
- homework policy and procedures
- homework folders or weekly folders procedures
- classroom rules and consequences (positive and negative)
- arrival and dismissal times
- how absences are handled, including how and when a student must make up the work missed
- schedules of special classes such as Art, Music, Media, and Physical Education
- list of necessary school supplies, including what *not* to bring to school
- what kinds of snacks to bring for snack time
- special classroom activities such as "Student of the Week," birthday celebration procedures and rules, and others
- special programs that are available at the school, such as speech, psychological, reading resource, and bilingual services
- list of extracurricular activities available at the school, including sports and clubs
- key calendar dates for the school year
- classroom parents committee information
- parent volunteer guidelines
- how you will communicate with parents (for example, newsletter, telephone calls, and notes)
- how a parent can contact you
- how a parent can request a conference with you

of any changes that need to be made, use what you now know as a frame of reference while completing steps three through seven.

Summary

Understanding what you expect from your teaching experience and what others' expect of you as a teacher helps prevent role conflict and role ambiguity, two major stressors for teachers. Becoming aware of the expectations *before* you begin your teaching assignment is key for effective stress prevention. Lastly, if you disagree with an expectation that is made of you, remember to be assertive and to try to resolve your differences in a proactive, amicable way.

Chapter 4

Step 3:
Know Your Resources

Knowing the resources that are available to you is the third step in helping you prevent stress. Being familiar with your resources helps you know what and who you can rely on and when. Teachers cite inadequate resources as one of their major stressors. If you are aware of any inadequacies ahead of time, you can take measures to deal with them in an assertive, proactive way. This avoids the stress you might get when you go to use a resource and find it isn't available.

Resources come in all shapes and sizes. They include time, people, and materials. The key is to know what resources exist and how to gain access to them.

You

You are your greatest resource. You are a source of energy, filled with creative ideas. Look beyond the obvious. You are capable of much more than you realize.

3.1   What are your strengths? What things can you do to capitalize on your strengths?

3.2   What are your weaknesses? What are some things you can do to improve them?

3.3   Where can you get help in learning how to unleash your creativity?

Time

Besides yourself, time is your next greatest resource. Perhaps it is so important to people because there never seems to be enough of it.

Teachers often cite a lack of time as their number one stressor. This stressor can make you feel overwhelmed, helpless, and out of control. An insufficient amount of planning time is usually a cause for this problem. The time you have for non-instructional duties is often very fragmented and filled with extra duties. With the loss of the large block of time needed for efficient planning, you might feel overwhelmed and less in control.

A True Story During my first year of teaching, I had thirty-five minutes of planning time, four days per week. Needless to say, this was not enough planning time, especially for a new teacher. As a result, a lack of time was a major stressor for me, and boy, was I stressed! Since then, I have learned to carve out more planning time within the timeframe I have been given. More on this topic in *Step 5: Create a Plan.*

To get a handle on this precious resource, it first needs to be analyzed. You must figure out how much time you have to spend and how it needs to be spent. First, identify any deadlines or events that direct your daily activities. Second, realize that you cannot control the passage of time, but you can control how you pass your time.

First, find out how much time you really have.

3.4 What is the school calendar (including holidays, half days, early release days, teacher workdays, open houses, and parent-teacher conference days)?

3.5 What is the calendar of school and school system events that involve you and your students (marking period dates, standardized testing dates, assemblies, picnics, field days, and vision/hearing/lice screenings)?

3.6 When is your first meeting with your grade level or department or team? When and how often are these meetings held?

3.7 What is your students' schedule for:
   a. art?
   b. music?
   c. physical education?
   d. media?
   e. other electives?

f. "academically gifted" programs?

g. "resource" programs?

h. recess and the use of the playground areas?

3.8 Can you help decide the schedule for the above special classes and programs?

3.9 What is your commitment schedule for:

a. extra duties?

b. extracurricular activities that you have already committed to do both inside and outside of school?

c. outside of school responsibilities (for example, daycare drop-off and pick-up times, your own children's soccer games schedule, and so forth)?

3.10 How much planning time do you have

a. during the days before the first day of school?

   i. Do you have any school system, school, grade level, or department meetings?

   ii. How much time do you have to spend in your classroom?

b. built into the school day?

c. on campus before and after school?

d. at home?

People

People, such as your colleagues, administrators, parents, and students, are invaluable resources to you. What you lack in skills and ideas, another person can have. Their strengths and weaknesses can compliment yours. By working together, your combined contributions can create something truly grand.

School Employees

School employees include your teaching colleagues, administration, office staff, and many others. These are people that can become true pillars of support for you and your students. Take a moment now to find out who they are.

3.11 Other teachers:

a. Who are your colleagues (at school and from other schools)?

   i. regular education teachers (note their grade levels or departments)

   ii. music teacher

   iii. art teacher

    iv.   media specialist (or librarian)

    v.   physical education teacher

    vi.   computer teacher

    vii.   foreign language teacher

    viii.   bilingual resource teacher

    ix.   reading specialists

    x.   special educators

    xi.   speech therapists

    xii.   occupational therapists

    xiii.   school psychologist

    xiv.   social worker

    xv.   school guidance counselor

    xvi.   curriculum specialist or instructional resource teacher

  b. What are their job descriptions and responsibilities?

  c. How can they help you and your students?

3.12 Is peer coaching available? How does one get involved?

3.13 Is team teaching available? How does one get involved?

3.14 Mentor:

  a. If you are assigned a mentor, with what things can she help you?

  b. If you are not assigned a mentor, with whom can you establish a mentor/ mentee type of relationship?

3.15 Do you have a teacher assistant (paid or unpaid)?

  a. How many hours or days per week is she assigned to your class?

  b. What are her job descriptions and responsibilities?

  c. Are there any legal constraints with respect to her responsibilities in the classroom?

  d. What is her teaching and discipline philosophies?

  e. Have you discussed your teaching program and her role in your program?

  f. Have you trained her in the tasks for which she is responsible?

  g. In what ways can you show her that you appreciate her help?

A True Story I once had a full time teacher assistant. She was a certified teacher with many years of experience. I learned a lot about teaching from just watching her work with my students. To me, she became more than an assistant; she became a good friend and a trusted mentor.

3.16 How can the following people support you and help you grow as a professional teacher?

   a. school administrators

   b. central office personnel

3.17 Other school staff:

   a. Who is on the following staffs at your school?

      i. office (including the school secretary and receptionist)

      ii. cafeteria

      iii. custodial

      iv. after hours janitorial service

      v. nursing

      vi. security

   b. What are their responsibilities?

   c. How do they help you and your students?

      i. When can you call on them for help?

      ii. Do they sponsor any contests or programs for you and your students?

   d. How can you help them do their jobs?

Your Students and Their Families

Now take a look at your own students, their siblings, and their parents. They are resources that go virtually untapped in many classrooms. To keep the information about these resources handy, you might want to set up a folder or card file for each of your students, noting the following pertinent information about them and their parents.

3.18 What is your class record (including names, addresses, telephone numbers, and parents' work telephone numbers)?

3.19 Your students:

   a. Who are your students?

b. Where are your students' confidential, permanent records kept? How and when can you get access to them? From these records (and additional information you gather after meeting them):

   i. What are their strengths and weaknesses?

   ii. What are their lives like outside of school?

   iii. What are their wants and needs as individuals? as a group?

   iv. What are their interests as individuals? as a group?

   v. What hobbies or expertise can they contribute and share with their classmates?

Parents are one of your greatest resources, and they often are underutilized. The use of parent volunteers is common in the lower grades, especially in kindergarten. However, the involvement wanes as students get older. It is important to keep parents involved throughout their children's school career because it has been found that higher parental involvement usually produces higher student achievement. Also, if you do not make the time and effort to get parents involved, you are losing an invaluable resource.

3.20 Your students' parents:

a. Who are your students' parents?

b. What hobbies or expertise can they contribute and share with your classes? (See appendix F for a sample parent survey you can use to collect this information.)

c. Which parents are more supportive of your students and of your class as a whole?

3.21 What ways does your school and district provide for parents (working and non-working) and community members (such as elderly folks, older siblings, or business owners) to:

a. get involved in your school and in your class? Is there an organized PTA or "classroom parents" program already in place? How does it work?

b. be informed of school system, school, or classroom happenings?

c. contribute or donate supplies, items, money?

d. be recognized and thanked for their contributions that enriched your classes' learning experiences? Are gifts purchased for them? By whom and with which funds?

3.22 What else can you do to support all of these efforts to involve parents and community members?

3.23 In what ways can older and younger students in your school assist you and your students (for example, as cross-age tutors, as helpers for younger students during dismissal, or as buddy classes)?

Support Programs and Services

People are the foundation of support programs and services. There are support programs and services both inside and outside of school.

Inside Your School

In a school system, programs and services exist for you and your students. Find out which ones are available.

3.24 What support programs (such as help lines and buddy programs) or services are in place for teachers? How does a teacher get access to them?

3.25 What programs and services (such as tutoring or mentor programs) are available for students who need extra help or extra enrichment? How does a student get access to them?

3.26 Is there a school based or school system based team (such as a Student Support Team, a Pupil Review Team, or a Student Assistance Team) that can assist you in determining better educational strategies to support the students who you might have a difficult time reaching?

    a. What is the name of this team?

    b. Who is on the team?

    c. What is the procedure for referring a student to this team?

    d. Do you need to document the teaching strategies you have been using with this student? Are you required to document these strategies for a certain period of time, such as six weeks, before referring a student?

    e. What forms, if any, do you need to complete before the meeting?

    f. Are parents invited to attend the meeting? Who sends the invitation?

    g. In what ways can they help you and your student?

A True Story The procedures for referring students to many of these school based assistance teams can be confusing. Over the years I have been a member of two different assistance teams and have referred students to two additional teams. Although each team's mission was similar, each had slightly different rules and procedures. I realized that it was a good idea to find out ahead of time how my school's assistance team operated before I ever needed their help. This proactive approach helped save a lot of time (and stress) when the need for their assistance arose.

3.27 Support for your classroom:

    a. Does someone clean your classrooms?

        i.   Who is it?

        ii.   How often?

        iii.   What is cleaned?

    b. If something is broken, what is the procedure for getting it repaired?

    c. If you need to, can you get access to your classroom over the weekend? How?

Outside Your School

There are also support programs for you and your students outside of the school system. For you, there are teacher associations, organizations, and agencies available. See appendix G for names and addresses of many such teacher resources. For your students, a school counselor or social worker might be very helpful in pointing out which educational, social, recreational, and cultural programs and services exist for them.

3.28 What teaching associations, organizations, and agencies are available?

3.29 What programs and services outside of the school system are available for your students?

3.30 Are any awards or contests in your county, state, or country available for

    a. your students?

    b. your school?

    c. you?

Support programs and services also exist for linking your classroom with others.

3.31 Are there opportunities to connect with other schools to work together on projects?

3.32 Are intra-school, inter-school, and U.S. Postal Service services available for you and your students to use? What are the procedures for:

    a. intra-school mail?

    b. inter-school mail?

    c. U.S. Postal Service mail?

Teaching Tools and Materials

It's hard to think about a teacher without conjuring up the images of a piece of chalk, a blackboard, a ruler, or a globe. These tools and materials are the hallmark of teaching, but there are many more.

When a classroom is not equipped with the tools and materials needed for teaching and learning, it becomes a stressor. In order to prevent this from happening, you must know what tools and materials are available for your and your students' use. Money is an issue in this category. Because of this, you might never have all of the tools and materials you feel are necessary to do your job. This is where you need to tap yourself and those around you for creative ideas to obtain or create the tools and materials you want and need for teaching your students.

First, look at the obvious. As soon as you receive your classroom key, take an inventory of what is in your classroom (if you have one). Use the "Equipment and Curriculum Materials Inventory" in the accompanying plan book, *7 Steps to Stress Free Teaching Plan Book*, to record this information. You can also use a plain sheet of paper to record the equipment (with their serial numbers) and the curriculum materials that are assigned to you and your classroom. Keep this information with your plan book so that the list of available tools and materials is always at your fingertips when you plan. Then, search beyond the obvious. Seek out those people you identified above who can help you find the tools and materials available at your school.

What Your School Provides

First, find out what items your school supplies for you and for your students. Begin by getting the most important items—your curriculum guides or standard course of study.

3.33 Where can you get copies of the curriculum guides or standard course of study for the classes you are teaching?

3.34 What diagnostic tests and tools are available for assessing your students' needs, achievement, interests, and attitudes?

3.35 Books:

    a. Which textbooks, basal reading series, and so forth, does the school or school system use?

    b. Are you required to use them?

    c. How do you get them?

    d. Are you responsible for issuing and accounting for your students' textbooks?

    e. Are you responsible for collecting your students' textbooks at the end of the school year?

    f. Where do you get the teacher's guides and other supplementary materials provided by the publisher for these books, if they exist?

    g. Are any books shared among teachers or students? Which ones?

    h.   May you order additional or different books?

         i.   From where are you authorized to purchase them?

        ii.   Who pays for them?

      iii.   What is the procedure for ordering them?

    i.   Are all of these books free of any gender, racial, ethnic, cultural, or age stereotypes? Are they free of any bias?

3.36 School supplies—consumable and non-consumable, including cleaning supplies, paid for with school funds (see appendix H for a list of possible supplies):

    a.   What school supplies are available for you and your students?

    b.   Do you get them from:

         i.   the grade level's or the department's supplies closet?

        ii.   the school's supplies closet?

      iii.   the school's or school system's warehouse?

      iv.   trade catalogs?

    c.   How do you get these supplies?

    d.   How long is the stock expected to last?

    e.   What are the procedures for reordering when stock is running low?

    f.   Are any of these supplies shared among teachers or students?

3.37 Are photocopiers, laminating machines, and overhead transparency makers available at your school or somewhere in your school system? What are the procedures, rules, and restrictions regarding their use?

A True Story Every laminating machine I have ever used needed to be "preheated" to a high temperature before it would work properly. I have gotten burnt (no pun intended!) many times because either I was too impatient to wait for it to get hot enough or someone accidentally turned it off before I got to use it. When the laminator is not hot enough, the plastic film does not adhere properly to the paper. As a result, you are left with something that comes apart over time. I have found that the worst situation is when the film partly adheres and you have to try to remove it with a straight pin without tearing your paper—a totally frustrating experience.

3.38 Computer technology and their peripherals (computer hardware, printers, modems, CD-ROM drives, and so forth):

    a.   What computer technology do you have access to:

         i.   for teaching?

        ii.   for your personal use?

b. What computer technology do your students have access to:

    i.   for learning?

    ii.   for their personal use?

c. Is there a computer lab for your class' use or for your students' personal use?

d. When can you and your students use the above technology? Is there a schedule?

e. What is your school's or school system's technology plan?

3.39   Do you or your students have Internet access? What is the procedure for obtaining an Internet account? Where can you go for help in learning about the Internet and what it has to offer?

3.40   Computer software programs/CDs/videos/laserdiscs/films/audiocassettes/ photographs/posters:

a. Which ones are available to you and your students through your school and school system?

b. What is the procedure for borrowing them?

c. Can you get them from retail stores? Who pays for them?

d. Do they come with teaching manuals that you can borrow?

e. Are all of these materials free of any gender, racial, ethnic, cultural, or age stereotypes? Are they free of any bias?

3.41   Other A/V Equipment (such as televisions, VCRs, overhead projectors, film projectors, filmstrip projectors, slide projectors, boom boxes, CD players, and headphones):

a. What audio/visual equipment (other than computer technology) do you have access to?

b. What is the procedure for getting this equipment?

c. Is this equipment shared among teachers and staff? Is there a schedule?

d. If you are assigned equipment, is it in proper working order equipped with emergency parts such as extra light bulbs and batteries?

3.42   Is your classroom or school equipped with a place where you can store your personal belongings, such as your coat, purse, and professional books?

3.43   Does your classroom or school have extra children's clothing on hand for students in case of any accidents?

A True Story One day one of my students was not feeling well and accidentally had a bowel movement in her pants. To compound her embarrassment, we did not have a change of clothes for her. Luckily, a teacher across the hall had a bag full of extra clothing. My student was able to borrow some clothes, and as a result, was able to save face with her peers. A similar embarrassing incident happened to a middle school student who began menses and was not prepared. The moral of the story: keep some extra clothes on hand, regardless of the age of your students.

3.44 What is the layout of your school building? Where are the bathrooms, water fountains, emergency exits, and so forth?

3.45 How do you sign up for the use of the cafeteria, multi-purpose room, and other large gathering rooms outside of your scheduled time?

What Your School System Provides

After you have done an exhaustive search in your school, look outward. Your school system might have a teacher's resource center or office stocked with extra teaching tools and materials. If your school system does not have one, perhaps there is one in your local area that is affiliated with your state's or county's teacher support system, such as the public university system.

3.46 Is there a teacher resource center available? Where is it located? When is it open?

Local Libraries

Use the public libraries. They are carrying more and more teaching related books and materials. Also visit local university libraries, especially those of schools that confer degrees in education. Their curriculum libraries have an abundance of materials.

3.47 What libraries are available for you to use and to borrow from?

    a. town or public libraries

    b. university or college libraries

A True Story I visit my public library a lot. Every few weeks I go to my public library and bring large canvas tote bags. I usually fill them with two to three dozen books I plan to read with my students over the following few weeks. Every time I go, I notice others checking out the same volume of books. Some even bring milk crates strapped onto hand trucks to make carrying the books easier. When I ask, I find out that these people are teachers, too—no surprise!

Your Colleagues

Borrowing from colleagues is another way to find the resources you might need. Your colleagues, especially those that have taught the same grade level or subject as you, usually have a wealth of resources already collected and organized. All it usually takes to get access to their resources is to simply ask. Many of your colleagues are probably extremely supportive and will share all that they have with you.

3.48 Who are the teachers who have taught your grade level or subject before?

Organizations

In addition to support, teaching associations and education agencies offer a lot of education related information (see appendix G for their names and addresses). They offer newsletters, periodicals, books, and other materials regarding effective teaching. Most of this information is packaged well and presented clearly.

You also have agencies and organizations that are not related to teaching who want to promote their missions or causes. They might also be sources of free or inexpensive materials that can be used in your lessons.

3.49 What are the teaching associations, organizations, and agencies that can help you obtain teaching tools and materials?

3.50 What are some other agencies and organizations that might have free or inexpensive materials that you can integrate into your lessons?

The Internet

The Internet is a powerful resource for you and your students. With Internet access, you have virtually an infinite amount of resources at your fingertips. It offers you and your students access to the latest information on any topic. It also offers you access to educational products and services (some of which are free) and access to hundreds of on-going discussion groups where teachers and students from around the world can interact and collaborate. In addition to on-line discussion groups, Internet e-mail also offers you and your students the opportunity to communicate quickly, easily, and inexpensively with other teachers and students from anywhere in the world. The possibilities are endless.

Because the Internet offers you and your students thousands of resources, using a search engine, such as Yahoo!®, with your Internet browser is one of the best ways to find what you are looking for. When you find a website that appears to be very useful or you are visiting it often, add a bookmark for it in your web browser. This saves you a lot of work the next time you want to access that particular website.

The Internet is dynamic. Thousands of websites are added everyday. At the same time, hundreds of other websites have address changes or are removed. As a result, it is futile to list all of the sites that could be helpful to you and your students. However, there are a few websites worth mentioning. For the latest educational research and news, good places to start include the U.S. Department of Education's website, any state's department of education websites, and the Educational Resources Information Center (ERIC) database website (see appendix I for more information about ERIC). A search engine can help you find these websites and others that can help you.

Learn about the Internet by taking classes and reading books and articles about it. Do not forget to ask your school's technology teachers about how this resource can become a tremendous asset to you and your students. The time spent learning is time well spent. It is worth it because the Internet brings an infinite amount of resources to you quickly and easily. Just as important, it links you to other teachers who have similar interests and problems. These teachers can become a part of your support network discussed in *Step 1: Take Care of Yourself*. This support network can help you solve problems, deal with stressors, and prevent stress.

    3.51   What are some useful Internet websites and discussion groups?

    3.52   Where can you go to learn more about the Internet and how to use it to help you in your teaching assignment?

One last note about the Internet: user beware! In addition to all of the good things on the Internet, there is also a huge amount of misinformation and unreliable data. Therefore, if you use the Internet to gather facts, proceed with caution and use common sense.

Sources of Additional Funds

Unfortunately, a lack of money is an issue in many schools. This forces teachers to find other means of obtaining needed and wanted resources. Grants, donations, earned bonus points from various book clubs, and free donations are just some of the ways you can get the resources you want and need.

There are many resources that list places where you can obtain free or very inexpensive teaching materials. Educators Progress Service, Inc. publishes books whose titles begin with the words *Educators Guide to Free...* (for example, *Educators Guide to Free Science Materials*). They are updated annually and sell out of stock fairly quickly. Several other books are also available and can be found at your local teaching supply store or bookstore. Professional teaching magazines, such as Scholastic's *Instructor* and The Education Center's *The Mailbox*®, are also very good sources of free and inexpensive materials. Check your media center to see if your school subscribes to these magazines.

Use the following questions to help you examine these options:

    3.53 Grants:

        a. How do you find out about which grants are available?

        b. What are the school's rules and procedures for applying for them?

3.54 Which book clubs can you join that also have bonus point systems?

     a. children's book clubs (such as Troll or Scholastic)

     b. adult book clubs (such as Doubleday Select, Inc.)

3.55 Are there any computer user groups that you can join for mutual support?

3.56 Are there any places or organizations that give away free materials?

3.57 Are donations (monetary or other), free presentations, and free tours available from:

     a. parents?

     b. local businesses?

Whenever asking for donations, be specific about what you want and why. If you aren't, you might end up with material that is of no use to you. You will then be responsible to store it or to dispose of it properly. Try to time the request appropriately and emphasize its educational purpose. Also emphasize the possibility that it could be a tax deductible donation. Finally, remember to send thank you notes after receiving any donations.

Recycle

Comb the yellow pages for businesses that discard items you might find useful. This is a great way for businesses to recycle what they can no longer use. For example, contact your local supermarket for paper and plastic bags, styrofoam trays, and clean cardboard cartons. Ask you local newspaper for unsold newspapers. Also, contact the carpet store for carpet remnants and contact the paint and wallpaper store for old wallpaper books. The carpets can be used to create a wonderful sitting area in your classroom and the wallpaper is great for making book covers. Again, be specific about the items you would like and be willing to explain what you will be doing with them.

Your last resort might be to simply look through the garbage. Yes, the garbage. There are several ones you should consider sifting through.

First, there is your own. Go through your closets. Find anything that you think you could recycle into something useful for your class. For example, take old dress shirts and use them as painting smocks. Do not throw away those fabric scraps! Use them for making book covers for student-authored books.

Next, check your school's garbage. There might be old teacher's manuals, old workbooks, and the like, especially if your school has recently adopted a new textbook series. Clean boxes and other storage type items in your school's garbage might also be good things to save. Be creative.

3.58 What are some things that you might be able to turn garbage (unwanted items) into?

Last Resort: Your Own Funds

If you must use your own money or are lucky enough to get an allowance from the school, try to invest in items that are nonconsumable, sturdy, and adaptable for meeting the needs of different students. Large discount stores, thrift stores, and garage sales are often good sources for such items and the prices are usually very affordable.

3.59   What things can you do to keep your personal spending down to a minimum when obtaining tools and materials that you cannot get in any other way?

A True Story There is a teacher who built a classroom library by purchasing books at garage sales. In one year, she purchased over three hundred, good condition books by attending garage sales, and most of the books were bought for less than $.50!

Summary

Resources are all around you. Find out as much as you can about them so that inadequate resources does not become a major stressor for you.

To be able to continually find new and better resources for you and your students, keep your eyes and ears open at all times. Most of all, keep an open mind.

Chapter 5

Step 4:
Determine the Goals

In *Step 1* through *Step 3*, you laid the foundation for preventing teacher stress. If you were building a house, the next step would be to lay down the joists that will support the ground floor. Using this analogy, your goals are the joists. In this step, you apply the answers from steps one through three and determine the goals for the school year.

Personal Goals

In *Step 1: Take Care of Yourself* and in *Step 2: Understand the Expectations*, you examined your wants and needs. Now clarify your personal goals. They are addressed first because of their importance in helping you take control of your life, a key ingredient for preventing stress.

Look at your whole life and examine your teaching assignment. What do you want to accomplish this year? Look at where you are and where you want to go. What do you want to accomplish in your life? Answer the following questions.

    4.1   What are your personal goals for the following areas of your life:

          a.   physical health

          b.   family and friends

c. spiritual

d. hobbies and interests

4.2 What are your professional goals?

    a. What grade and subject do you want to teach?

    b. What image do you want your students, parents, colleagues, and administrators to have of you?

    c. How do you want to be remembered by your former students?

In addition to the broad professional goals you have now recorded, you might also have more specific professional goals. For example, this year you might want to learn more about using technology as a teaching tool or you might want to become more involved in a professional teaching organization or association. Answer the following questions.

4.3 What do you want to learn about this year?

4.4 Are there any professional teaching organizations or associations in which you would like to become more involved?

Your professional goals also include the things you would like to do with your class this year. All of your teaching experiences thus far have helped shape your opinions about what does and what does not work for you and your students. As a result, you might have ideas about activities that you want to do this year.

4.5 Are there any activities you have done in the past that you would like to do again this year? like to change this year? not like to do at all this year?

4.6 Is there something new that you want to try this year with your students?

A True Story Every year I make new distinctions about what works in the classroom. In addition, I know that what works with one group of students does not always work with another group. Yet, I am always eager to try new things. One such example is using learning centers in the classroom. I had used centers effectively as a primary grade teacher. However, in every school where I taught upper elementary grade levels, I found that centers were rarely used at these grade levels. As a result, I decided to make centers an integral part of my third through fifth grade classes one year. I read many professional resources and spoke with other teachers about how they managed centers in their classroom. Using my primary grades teaching experience and some of the new ideas I had learned, I successfully integrated learning centers into my classes. The centers enhanced my teaching and improved my students' achievement.

Your Goals for Your Students

"My students will become lifelong learners." "My students will get accepted into college." "My students will learn the multiplication tables." These are all excellent goals to strive for, but you have to ask yourself if these are goals you are expected to achieve. Perhaps they are. Perhaps they are not, and they are just reflections of your personal goals for your students. Having student goals that are not supported by your employer can be a cause for role ambiguity and role conflict. So, be careful.

Remove any role ambiguity and role conflict by making sure you help your students reach the goals you were hired to help them achieve. If you choose to work towards different goals, you might place unnecessary pressure on yourself and on your students. Unnecessary pressure can lead to unwanted stress.

The simplest way to find the required goals is to consult your curriculum guides, standard course of study, grade level proficiency lists, or scope and sequence charts. They should consist of cognitive, affective, and psychomotor goals for your students. If they do not exist or are incomplete, ask your colleagues, your principal, or your school system curriculum administrators. If there are no curriculum goals for your teaching assignment, find out the state and national guidelines, including standards and guidelines from national councils such as the National Council of Teachers of Mathematics (NCTM), the National Council of Teachers of English (NCTE), and others.

4.7 Using all of the curriculum guides or other curriculum documents for your assigned teaching positions,

   a. which parts of the curriculum are you responsible to teach?

   b. what are your curriculum goals?

If there are any parts of the curriculum documents that appear vague, ask your principal and colleagues for clarification. For example, if they state students must learn to write legibly but do not specify the exact style of handwriting, find out from your principal or colleagues which style the school or district recommends that you teach.

Unfortunately, it is not enough to identify curriculum goals based solely upon the curriculum documents. You also need to look at your students. You might be assigned students that have either not achieved the prerequisite skills needed to be successful in your class or have already achieved the goals you have outlined above. In these cases, you might need to modify some of the goals on your list for some of your students. The goals you establish must be appropriate for each student that you teach.

Examine your students' permanent records and identify any students that might need modified goals. Any student that has an Individualized Education Plan (IEP), or equivalent, probably needs modified or additional goals.

4.8   Are there any curriculum goals that need to be modified for your students?

    a.   Which students?

    b.   Which goals need modification?

    c.   Are any additional goals needed for these students?

Climate Goals

To prevent stress, you also need to establish a classroom climate that helps you prevent stress. Climate is all about relationships. It is the emotional health of the relationships among a group of people. Climate, therefore, is the atmosphere or tone created by the emotional health of the relationships that exist among the members of your classroom and those that exist between your classroom and everyone else. As the teacher, you have tremendous control over your classroom's climate.

Discipline problems, cited as one of the major stressors for most teachers, plays a significant role in classroom climate. Discipline problems result when students use inappropriate behaviors to deal with a demand or expectation placed upon them. Students feel pressured into a corner and try to get out whichever way they know how—from fighting to daydreaming. Discipline problems erode the emotional health of those involved and of bystanders. These problems become a strain on the classroom's climate. When they occur, you need to have the skills to deal with the inappropriate behavior. Many of these skills are discussed in the next chapter. There are also several resources you can use to learn these skills. Check your school's professional library and stores that sell teacher resources for a wealth of these kinds of resources.

As the classroom leader, you have the power to create a climate that can help you prevent stress. Use the following questions to help you identify your climate goals and to determine if you are committed to this very important stress prevention strategy.

4.9   What is your current classroom climate like or what has your past classroom climate been like?

4.10   What are your climate goals for this school year?

4.11   What are your school's climate goals? How do your climate goals support the school's climate goals?

Summary

If the steps for preventing stress were compared to the steps for building a home, determining the goals would be like laying down the joists for the ground floor. In this step, you have laid down the joists by outlining goals for yourself, for your students, and for your classroom climate. These goals are the input needed to complete the ground floor of the house—your plan.

Chapter 6

Step 5:
Create a Plan

The ground floor of a home is supported by the joists below it. The goals you outlined in *Step 4: Determine the Goals* are like the joists. Just as the ground floor of a home must be connected to the joists below it, your plan must be connected to your goals.

Step 5: Create a Plan is the step where everything you have done in the previous four steps gels together. This chapter serves as a guide to help you orchestrate all of the pieces that are needed in an effective stress prevention plan. The pieces include schedules, unit plans, and classroom climate.

Schedules—Making Time to Achieve All of Your Goals

Before you begin to schedule everything that goes into a plan, consider the following guidelines.

- Keep a steady, comfortable pace; do not try to do everything in one day.
- Use time wisely, especially the hours you are at school.
- Build buffers into your schedule to accommodate unforeseen delays to help ensure you meet deadlines.
- Coordinate personal and school events so that you are not involved in too many highly stressful situations at once.

- Stay as organized as you can to help you feel less overwhelmed and more in control of your time.

- Be flexible and understand that you might need to rearrange your schedule as the days and weeks go by.

Your Personal Activities

Photocopy "Your Personal Schedule" on page 82 and on page 83 and mark the times you need to be at school. After blocking out the time you are required to be at work and the time needed to travel to and from work, schedule the personal activities needed to fulfill your personal goals. Schedule your personal life as carefully as you schedule your lesson plans. Although you might have to adjust this schedule as the year progresses, mark them in now so that personal plans get the priority they need.

Include as many personal activities as you know of at this time. Some of the activities to consider scheduling now are the time needed for sleeping, for eating properly, and for exercising. Also mark in the time you want to set aside for family and friends, spiritual growth, hobbies, extracurricular activities (yours and your children's, especially if you have to drive them to and from these activities), and professional development activities. After you have set aside time for all of the above, make sure you schedule some time to just relax—"me-time." This is time to do whatever you please and however you please.

A True Story Teaching is not just a job, it is a profession. Whether you want to or not, you usually take work home with you. This work can be papers to grade or just thoughts. Teaching is a kind of work that is hard to "turn off." When I began teaching, it was very hard to separate my work from my personal life. As a result, my family time and my "me-time" was virtually all taken up by my work. This was not good. I was very stressed and within a few months, I felt completely burnt out. In the years that followed, I made time for me and my family. I scheduled it. Although it was not possible to follow my exact schedule everyday, I was able to follow it most of the time. As a result, my stress decreased sharply. I became a much happier person and a much more effective teacher.

Your School Calendar

Second, obtain a copy of your school's calendar. Using the "Schedule of School Events" in the *7 Steps to Stress Free Teaching Plan Book* and the weekly lesson plan pages in your plan book, denote which days are vacation days, holidays, half days, teacher work days, open houses, parent teacher conferences, marking period dates, and any other kinds of special days that are identified on the calendar. Do not forget to include other special school or school system events that involve you and your students, even if they are not listed on your school's calendar. Appendix J has additional special days that you might want to include. After you are through transferring the dates, tape your school calendar to the inside back cover of your plan book to use as a handy reference during the school year.

Your Students' Schedules

Third, if you are a teacher of a self-contained class, obtain a schedule of your class' special times such as lunch, Art, Music, and so forth (a complete list can be found in *Step 3: Know Your Resources*) and a schedule of your students' pull out resource and enrichment schedule. Record these student schedules on the "Daily Schedules for Students" page in the *7 Steps to Stress Free Teaching Plan Book* or on a blank page in your plan book for easy reference. Also record these schedules in the first two weeks of your plan book pages. Save yourself a lot of work by not copying this information on the rest of your plan book's pages until the schedule is solid. This might take several weeks because these schedules often change in the first few of weeks of school, especially in high growth communities where higher student registration than expected creates many last minute changes in classes and in schedules.

Your Teaching Schedule

Fourth, obtain the schedule for your duties and meetings. If you teach several classes during the day, find out when you are required to teach and when you are required to do extra duties. You also need to obtain the schedule of any weekly meetings in which you are involved. Like your students' schedules, only denote these times on the first two weeks of your plan book pages to save yourself work if the schedules should change soon after school starts. With these times denoted, you have an idea of how much time you have for planning.

Examine Your Planning Time

Compare "Your Personal Schedule" with your teaching schedule in your plan book. Identify all of your planning time—a crucial element in preventing stress.

5.1   How much time do you have for planning? When is it?

5.2   What time of day are you most alert and energetic? Is there a way to make your planning time coincide with your "best time"?

If possible, adjust your schedules to accommodate your best time. This is the first step in helping you to maximize the use of your time. Maximizing the use of your time helps you prevent stress.

Unit Plans—How to Achieve the Goals You Have Outlined for Your Students

Excellent unit plans help you prevent stress. They prevent stress because they keep your students interested and on task which prevents student discipline problems, a major stressor. Excellent unit plans also help your students be successful, which in turn makes them, their parents, and your administrators very happy. Therefore, it is important to learn how to create excellent unit plans within the planning time you identified above.

Your Personal Schedule

Time	Sunday	Monday	Tuesday	Wednesday
6:00 am				
6:30				
7:00				
7:30				
8:00				
8:30				
9:00				
9:30				
10:00				
10:30				
11:00				
11:30				
12:00 pm				
12:30				
1:00				
1:30				
2:00				
2:30				
3:00				
3:30				
4:00				
4:30				
5:00				
5:30				
6:00				
6:30				
7:00				
7:30				
8:00				
8:30				

Your Personal Schedule

Time	Thursday	Friday	Saturday	Notes
6:00 am				
6:30				
7:00				
7:30				
8:00				
8:30				
9:00				
9:30				
10:00				
10:30				
11:00				
11:30				
12:00 pm				
12:30				
1:00				
1:30				
2:00				
2:30				
3:00				
3:30				
4:00				
4:30				
5:00				
5:30				
6:00				
6:30				
7:00				
7:30				
8:00				
8:30				

If you are a new teacher, creating unit plans is probably the skill in which you have the most training and in which you have the least amount of experience. If you are a veteran teacher, you might have a lot of experience in creating unit plans. Hopefully your experience has shown you how to create great unit plans efficiently. Whether you are just starting your teaching career or you have been teaching for years, the following is a brief review of how to create great unit plans.

Unit Plans—What They Are

Unit plans are not lesson plans. However, they do include lesson plans. Unit plans are developed topics or themes that teach several related goals over the course of a few days, a few weeks, or even a few months. The related goals might all be from one subject, such as mathematics, or they might be from two or more subjects, such as social studies and language arts. A table of contents for a unit plan consists of an introduction (a brief summary justifying the use of the topic or theme), goals and behavioral objectives, subject matter, possible methods of starting the unit, possible lesson activities, possible culminating projects, suggested methods of evaluation (formative and summative), resources, and lesson plans. As most veteran teachers agree, the more time and effort you put into these units up front, the more use you get out of them later on.

To help you prevent stress, develop only one or two units at this time, but create a skeleton framework for the entire year. Develop your behavioral objectives and lesson plans during the school year. Keep in mind, however, that many teachers recommend having lessons, with their associated materials and handouts, prepared at least one week in advance of the day you present it. Many teachers advise two weeks or more for preventing stress effectively.

Right now, just concentrate on completing steps 1 through 5 below. You map out the use of your future planning time in "Schedules—Another Look," the last section of this chapter, to accommodate the time to complete the remaining steps (which include lesson planning).

How to Create a Unit Plan

The following steps briefly outline one of the many ways for creating unit plans.

Step 1

Start with all of the student goals you identified in *Step 4: Determine the Goals*. Write each one a separate strip of paper. To save some time, photocopy the goals from your curriculum guides, standard courses of study, or learning results outlines (whichever your school system uses) if you can and cut out each one. Having them separate will be helpful later when you try to combine the goals into logical combinations.

Step 2

Using a large sheet of paper (bulletin board paper or butcher paper is helpful), create a chart with the different curriculum areas you are responsible to teach labeled across the top (this could be different subjects, such as math, science, and social studies, or it could be areas within a subject, such as counting, classification, and patterning, for the subject of mathematics). Down the left side, place the following three labels: content, skills, and attitudes. See the sample chart on page 85.

Complete the chart with your goals, placing them in the correct areas on your chart. After you have completed placing your goals on the chart, color code each goal using different colored markers identifying which curriculum area and which kind of goal it is. This saves time later when you check to see if your units are balanced.

Sample Chart

	Reading	Writing	Social Studies	Math	Science
Content					
Skills					
Attitudes					

Step 3

After your goals have been color coded, begin to make logical connections among the goals. Ask yourself the following:

5.3   Which goals would it make sense to teach together?

Most teachers find that many of the goals can be taught together very effectively because they are content, skills, and attitudes that are needed to answer a particular real life question. For example, several mathematics and science goals can be taught together. Some of the topics that cross both of these subjects are collecting, organizing, and displaying data. Therefore, a real life question that ties a particular science and mathematics unit together might be, "What are different ways to collect, organize, and display data?" A theme that might be used to answer this question is air and atmosphere. Another theme that could be used is rocks and minerals. The theme chosen is usually driven by the content goals that you identified in Step 2 above.

Notice that the theme is not the focus of your unit. The focus is the question. The question is the unifying element of all the goals in the unit. It also helps you determine which activities you plan to do in your unit. When shared with your students, it provides them with a meaningful reason to learn the content, skills, and attitudes outlined in your curriculum. It helps them see a purpose to what they are learning.

A True Story Creating a unit around a question is very different than what I used to do. I used to choose my themes first and then try to group a bunch of my goals into them, whether they fit together logically or not. I also used to think that I was integrating curriculum when I used plastic bear counters in a math lesson during my "bear unit." I have learned that what I was doing was just a cute idea, not integrating curriculum. Most important, I have learned that once you have made logical, real life connections among the goals and have created a unifying question, students must be told this question. The question becomes the driving force behind the unit because it stimulates thinking and motivates learning. The unifying question is an essential element of effective instruction.

As you combine your goals into logical groups, try to balance the groups with content, skills, and attitude goals so that one group does not have all content goals and another has all attitude goals. This helps keep your units balanced. Note that it does not matter if one unit has several more goals than another unit. The real measure of merit is whether the combination of goals makes sense.

After trying to see which goals logically fit together, you might end up with a handful of goals that really do not fit logically with any other goals. Do not force them to fit! Do not force illogical, meaningless, connections because it could weaken the strength of your unit. It is okay to teach some goals in isolation. An example might be learning the multiplication tables. If you find you have a handful of goals left over, just remember to make time to teach them.

5.4   Which goals just don't fit with any others and need to be taught separately?

Sequence the groups of goals and those that were left over into rough timeline. Note that some of your teaching resources from your school system might include pacing charts. Refer to them as you try to determine your timeline.

Step 4

Find out from your grade level or department colleagues if a list of reserved themes for your grade level or subject exists. If it does exist, you have a head start. Whether the list exists or not, collect your resources for the grade level or subject you teach. This includes teacher's manuals, textbooks, computer programs, and any other professional resources you can find for your grade level or subject.

If you do not have a list of themes, identify some possible themes from the clusters of goals you identified in Step 3. Also, peruse the resources you collected for reoccurring content themes or topics. Keep in mind your students' interests and developmental level. One way to figure out your students' interests is to put interesting, inviting books about different topics all around your classroom and ask your students to peruse the books. Notice which books and topics they naturally gravitate to. Keep in mind *your* interests and experience, too. If you are already interested in and familiar with a topic, it is easier for you to develop it into a unit plan. Also, keep in mind your school's, students parents', and community's philosophies and policies. Are there any themes or topics that are encouraged or discouraged? In addition, do not forget to find out if any themes or topics are reserved for other grade levels or departments. You don't want to step on anyone's toes!

Choose a sufficient number of themes for the entire school year. This number depends upon the grade level you teach. Ask your colleagues for some sort of number. If you still have no idea, begin with six to eight themes. Develop one or two before you start teaching your students. The others can be changed if your students' interests are different. If you teach all of the subjects, make sure there is a balance of social studies and science dominant themes.

    5.5   What is the rationale for the themes chosen?

           a.   Are they consistent with the curriculum and with the expectations?

           b.   Are the themes meaningful, interesting, and developmentally appropriate for your students?

Step 5

Once your themes have been determined, learn as much as you can about them. Check your libraries, the Internet—anything and anywhere. Check the children's literature section in your libraries. They have a wealth of information which has already been prepared for students, often making the topics easier to understand than adult non-fiction books on the same subject. Determine if there is enough unbiased information available on the topic. If not, you might want to see if there is a different theme that would be easier for you to develop into a unit plan. Also, if possible, find out what your students already know about the topic to help you save time. You can do a survey or do a KWL chart (what we "K"now, what we "W"ant to know, what we have "L"earned) with them.

    5.6   Are there enough quality resources available to create a unit plan for each of the themes? If not, what are other possible themes?

Step 6

Using everything you have learned about your themes, brainstorm some activities you could do with each of them. One way to generate ideas is to write down what you think of when you think of the particular theme. You can also write down what you would like to learn about the theme. At the same time, identify which curriculum goals can be achieved with each of these activities.

Step 7

Use the goals and activities to write behavioral objectives. A behavioral objective is a statement that has three parts. The three parts are a student's observable behavior (written as an action verb with a direct object), a condition that exists for the behavior to occur (such as the materials or learning strategies that are used), and a criteria that is used to determine minimally acceptable performance or achievement. An example of a behavioral objective is, "Using a graphic organizer, the student will categorize the different modes of transportation into at least three different categories." "Using a graphic organizer" is the condition, "categorize the different modes of transportation" is the observable behavior, and "at least three different categories" is the minimum criteria for acceptable performance. Keep in mind your students' IEP goals and objectives as you do this. Use the following question to assess your objectives.

5.7 Do the objectives cover all of the levels in Bloom's Taxonomy?

Step 8

Use behavioral objectives, which include the activities, goals, and evaluation criteria, as the framework for your lesson plans. If the objectives are clear, meaningful, and realistic, it is easy to write effective lesson plans. Effective lesson plans have high student success rates. Consequently, your students will also have higher achievement scores, better retention, and more positive attitudes toward school.

You might not always design an effective lesson. If this happens and you find that something is not working well during a lesson, be flexible and change it. Have a backup plan available and make a note on the lesson plan of what went wrong so that you do not repeat the same mistake the next time you do it.

The following are the essential parts of an effective lesson plan:
- time allotted for lesson
- goals
- behavioral objectives
- materials needed
- procedure of the lesson (includes review, a motivational introduction to get children involved early, development of the goals and objectives, supervised practice, independent practice, and homework assignment)
- ways in which you plan to give constructive feedback to your students (this is a must because if you recall from *Step 2: Understand the Expectations*, feedback is *the* teacher behavior that matters most for strong student achievement)
- closure
- assessment of achievement of goals (formative and summative)

While creating your lesson plans, be aware of how much time you have to do the lesson with your students. Also, make a note of how you group your students (whole group or small group). Remember to also add a note in your lesson plan to remind you to explain to students how they are assessed and any due dates for their independent assignments.

Assess the quality of your lesson plans with the following questions:

5.8 Have you provided a diversification in
   a. the types of activities?
   b. instructional strategies (including small and large group instruction)?
   c. teaching styles?
   d. matching different learning styles?
   e. supporting and strengthening multiple intelligences?

5.9 Do the activities keep students actively involved?

5.10 Is enough individualization provided to ensure success for all of your students?

5.11 Are the lessons interesting and worthwhile?

5.12 Do you create small groups of students for instruction or for certain activities?

    a. How are the groups determined (for example, by language or by ability)?

    b. How often are these groups used?

    c. How do the lists of members change and how often?

    d. Are these groups empowering or inhibiting for your students?

5.13 Assessment:

    a. Do your lessons have built in mechanisms or provide for manageable ways of collecting information needed for ongoing assessment or grades?

    b. Do the lessons give students the experience of different types of assessments, such as paper and pencil tests, presentations, portfolios, and others?

    c. How many grades or evaluations do you need to get a true picture of a student's achievement?

    d. Is the grading and evaluation practice you have chosen consistent with school policy?

5.14 Have you included information about what students should do if they finish the guided and independent assignments before their peers?

5.15 Do you have or want to have extra credit activities?

5.16 Do any of the lessons have potential points of failure? Is there anything in the lesson that can be changed so that this does not happen? If the lesson should not go as planned, is there a "plan B" available?

Step 9

Design pre-tests and post-tests for your goals of your unit. Pre-tests help determine whether your students have the prerequisite knowledge needed for the unit. Combined with post-tests, they help you quantify your students' growth and progress as a result of your unit. The test results also help you evaluate the effectiveness of your unit as a whole. See "Test Administration Tips" on page 90 for some ways to help you and your students prevent stress.

Note that at the beginning of the year, you need to do a special assessment of your students. You need to assess your students' achievement and retention of curriculum goals from the previous school year. You can use ready made diagnostic or achievement tests, or you can make your own using review items from textbooks and materials your students used the previous year. Analyzing your students' work samples from the previous year and from the first few days of school also gives you clues of their achievement to date. Making observations, conducting interviews, and administering interest and attitude surveys are additional ways to assess your students.

Test Administration Tips

Giving tests is just one way to assess achievement. Use these test administration tips to help you and your students prevent stress during these traditionally stressful moments.

Before giving the test:

- Prepare students for the test by giving them the test date and any review material they might need several days in advance.
- Schedule the test well in advance of any grade reporting deadlines in order to have enough time to correct the tests.

During the test:

- Make sure students are comfortable and have enough elbow room.
- Seat students away from people that might pressure them to rush through their test.
- Schedule enough time to give the test so you and your students do not feel pressured by time constraints.
- Tell them how much time they have to complete the test.
- Review what you expect them to do in case of a fire drill or other type of interruption.
- Explain the ramifications if they are caught cheating.
- Review how they should ask for help during the test if they need it.
- Review what to do if they finish the test early.
- Wait until there are no more questions before handing out the test.

Step 10

Both you and your students should do a summative evaluation of the unit.

Your students should write (if developmentally appropriate) about the parts of the unit they feel were the best and the worst and why they feel this way. This gives you insight as to what to alter for next time. They can also give you some ideas about activities that you might want to add to the unit.

You, too, need to reflect upon the unit. Make notes of these things before you put the unit back on the shelf. Ask yourself the following questions:

5.17 What do you think went well and was effective? Which lessons are worth repeating? Which need some work? Which need to be scrapped?

5.18 Was the unit fun for you and for your students?

5.19   Was the unit focused and teachable?

5.20   Did the unit have a wide variety of activities?

With your unit plans created, it is time to design a plan for establishing your classroom's climate.

Achieving Your Climate Goals

Climate is the atmosphere created by the emotional health of the relationships that exist among the members of your classroom and of those that exist between your classroom and everyone else. Remember that as the teacher, you have tremendous control over your classroom's climate, and consequently, a lot of control over whether you achieve your climate goals.

As the leader of your classroom, almost everything you do impacts the climate. Climate is most affected by how you manage your and your students' interpersonal relationships. These relationships are further impacted by how you manage your classroom's physical environment and your time.

The First Few Days of School

Climate is predominantly established in the first few days of school. Therefore, as you read the rest of this section, keep in mind that most of the suggestions made should be planned for or done before school starts. If this is not possible, make an extra effort to do these things within the first few weeks of school. Remember, the more you do ahead of time, the better. It gives you greater control during the first few days of school, the most critical time of the school year for establishing a positive climate.

Interpersonal Relationships

The most important thing that affects climate is the tone of the interpersonal relationships that exist inside and outside your classroom. If you want to prevent stress, you need to become an effective manager of the interpersonal relationships that exist within your classroom and of the relationships between your class and everyone else.

You can manage interpersonal relationships in two ways. One way is to manage the relationship in real time, as it happens. The other is to manage it ahead of time, by planning different ways to ensure that any interpersonal interactions are positive. Look at the interpersonal relationships that exist within your classroom and the relationships between your class and everyone else in these two ways.

Relationships Within Your Classroom

The interpersonal relationships within your classroom consume most of your day. Therefore, it is very important that this part of your plan is very thorough. There are key things you can do to successfully manage the relationships within your classroom.

Monitor Your Behavior. Since you have total control over yourself, act sincerely and eliminate things that you do or say that could become stressors for your students. Some of these things include having inadequate classroom management skills, having unprepared lessons, being disorganized, having unclear goals, showing inconsistent behavior, being sarcastic, and showing no empathy.

Build Rapport. The easiest way to accomplish this is to treat your students with respect. Be fair, nurturing, firm, and consistent. Allow mistakes and help your students learn from them. Do not react to inappropriate behavior. Instead, respond in a professional, supportive manner.

There are some simple behaviors that you can do in order to increase rapport in your classroom. They include:

- using an open body posture
- smiling
- using eye contact
- using your students' names when addressing them
- giving students choices
- listening actively

The rapport you build helps you gain their respect and cooperation, removing another common stressor for teachers.

Satisfy the Basic Need for Security. Make your students feel safe and secure in their environment. This is accomplished by being accepting of all of your students, no matter who they are or how they act. One way your students get this message is by acknowledging their feelings by saying things like, "You are frustrated with school," as opposed to saying, "When I was your age,...." It is also accomplished by being tolerant of each child's individuality and by avoiding sarcasm. It is also important to help your students understand what they are supposed to be doing at all times and to compliment students on their achievements.

Create a Sense of Belonging. All of your students must learn that they belong to a group and that they have responsibilities to the group. Conduct class meetings to show them how and when their actions have an effect upon the group and upon the school. Make every student feel she is an important part of the class by creating a team atmosphere. To foster a team atmosphere, explain and model citizenship, especially courtesy, and expect it from your students at all times. Do activities, found in many team building resources, to build mutual support among your students, and use cooperative learning strategies to teach them how to cooperate with one another.

A True Story To help foster team spirit, a third grade teacher adopted a catchy team name and a mascot. This teacher, "Mrs. Brown," named her class "Mrs. Brown's Bears" and chose the bear as their class mascot. The room was decorated with bears, from nametags in the shape of bears to stuffed teddy bear accessories. This team identity fostered a sense of belonging and a sense of security for the members of her class.

5.21   What can you do to build rapport with your students, to satisfy your students' need for security, and to create a sense of community in your classroom? What personal changes do you need to make in order to do these things?

Prevent Discipline Problems. As discussed in the last chapter, discipline problems can erode a classroom's climate. Preventing discipline problems helps to eliminate this problem.

Hitting, fighting, cheating, and stealing are some behaviors that most teachers believe are never appropriate under any situation. However, other "inappropriate" behaviors, such as talking, can be appropriate within the proper setting. Remember, many times it isn't what the student is doing that is inappropriate, it is the time that the student chooses to engage in that behavior that is inappropriate.

Sometimes the inappropriate behaviors result from inappropriate expectations of students (social, emotional, and academic), from poor interpersonal relationships, and from poor classroom management—all signs of ineffective teaching. Sometimes no matter how much you try to prevent inappropriate behavior, it still occurs. When it does, you need to have the skills to handle it. Never react, but respond to the situation. Keep your cool and remember to acknowledge the student's feelings. Often times this goes a long way in diffusing the problem.

In addition to being prepared to handle discipline problems, another way to prevent stress is to do as much as possible to help prevent discipline problems from ever occurring in the first place. To prevent discipline problems, build classroom management skills that help foster desirable student behavior. These management skills include the following:

- **With-it-ness (Being Alert):**
  being aware of everything that is going on in the room at all times so you can reinforce appropriate behavior and can stop minor problems before they become major ones.

- **Overlapping:**
  handling more than one activity or problem at the same time by paying attention to the important aspects of everything going on around you. This prevents you from becoming overwhelmed and from getting sidetracked.

- **Movement Management:**
  pacing activities appropriately and transitioning between activities effectively, including giving clear beginnings (such as "Begin now.") and clear endings (such as "Stop working now.") to activities and not starting new activities until you have all of your students' attention. It also includes establishing classroom routines and procedures that bring structure and smoothness to your classroom (discussed later in this chapter).

- **Group Alerting:**
  keeping all students involved in the task at hand and getting non-responders to participate.

- **Specific Praise:**
  giving students praise which is believable and which tells them exactly what they did well or did correctly. An example is, "You remembered to put your name on the top of your paper so I could see who did the work. Super!" Specific praise must be true and the student must believe you. Specific praise should be given for correct academic responses as well as for appropriate behavior. Note that sometimes specific praise works better if it is delivered only loud enough for the student receiving the praise to hear it. If other students hear the praise,

they might reject the student or make fun of him. This might create discipline problems which can erode the relationships in your class.

- **Encouragement:**
  giving students a nonjudgmental approval focused on the task, process, product, or behavior, and not on the student (such as "This essay is excellent!"); an encouraging comment (such as "Let's look at it this way..." and "Keep at it!"); and a feedforward direction (such as "This sentence needs a punctuation mark." and "Use rule #3 here.").

To manage discipline problems as they occur, you can use some of the strategies listed above plus the following:

- **Planned Ignoring:**
  choosing not to *appear* to pay attention to a student involved in a minor misbehavior while maintaining your own and other students' focus to the task at hand and not on the inappropriate behavior. It also includes waiting for the student to begin engaging in an appropriate behavior and praising the appropriate behavior immediately after you observe it.

- **Physical Proximity:**
  while continuing to teach, walking over to stand near someone who is behaving inappropriately. Involves remaining focused on the task at hand while using your physical presence to let the student know you have noticed what she is doing. This if often used with planned ignoring, specific praise, gestural warning/reminders, or mild desists.

- **Gestural Warnings/Reminders:**
  briefly using eye contact, a stern look, or pointing to posted classroom rules or to the task material to let a student know you are aware of her behavior and to remind the student of what she is supposed to be doing.

- **Mild Desists (Soft Reprimands):**
  telling a student to stop the inappropriate behavior or telling the student what to do to start behaving appropriately. Because publicly made reprimands usually backfire, mild desists are effective when given in a calm, firm tone of voice loud enough only for the student to hear.

- **Negative Reinforcement:**
  creating an undesirable condition students can avoid if they behave appropriately.

If these teacher behaviors do not work to decrease or eliminate the inappropriate behavior, then you can try the following:

- **Token Economy:**
  creating a reward system whereby students earn points, tickets, or some other symbolic token for appropriate behavior that can be used to "purchase" a pre-determined prize, such as an activity, item, or privilege, at a later time. This requires a list of exactly what students must do to earn the tokens (usually different amounts of tokens can be earned for different types of behaviors) and a list of what the tokens can purchase (usually different amounts for different "prizes").

- **Contracts:**
  students, teachers, and sometimes also parents signing a written agreement that specifies what particular privilege or reward the student earns if he engages in a particular behavior.

- **Response Cost:**
  taking away a privilege, activity, or item a student already has if the student behaves inappropriately (for example, taking away recess privileges for breaking a classroom rule).

- **Time-out (Social Isolation):**
  briefly removing a student from the situation and isolating him from other people and materials for short lengths of time. Use this method cautiously.

The figure, "Teacher Attributes that Can Help Prevent Discipline Problems," shows some other attributes a teacher should possess to help prevent discipline problems.

Teacher Attributes that Can Help Prevent Discipline Problems

A teacher's personality traits can help prevent discipline problems. Which ones do you have? Which ones should you work on developing?

Approachability
Businesslike behavior
Consistency
Dependability
Enthusiasm and Empathy
Fairness
Genuineness
Humor
Interest in children
Just decisions
Kindness
Listening to children
Mutual respect
Nags not
Openness
Patience and Positive regard for children
Quiet manner
Respect for children
Supportiveness
Teaching appropriate behavior step by step
Understanding
Valuing learning
Withitness
eXpectation that children behave appropriately
Yells not
Zeroes in on causes of misbehavior

From *Beyond Student Teaching* by Ellen Kronowitz; Copyright © 1992. Reprinted by permission by Addison Wesley Longman, Inc.

5.22 Which classroom management skills do you need to develop or improve? How and when do you plan to develop or improve them?

Keep Students on Task. Things you can do to keep students on task during a lesson include calling on students randomly to answer questions, having materials for your lesson prepared ahead of time, asking all of the students to answer in unison, and using ways for each student to become actively involved in a lesson. Also, make sure that all assignment directions and behavior expectations have been stated clearly and are understood by all students. Keep students on task by keeping them motivated with high, yet reasonable, standards for achievement.

To help keep students on task while they work independently on an assignment, circulate around the classroom, check students' work and progress, and give them specific feedback about their work. One way to accomplish this efficiently and effectively is to use the "praise, prompt, leave" method described by Steere. As you pass a student, praise them for their hard work and effort, prompt them by stating what they should do next, and leave. An example of a prompt is telling them to check a particular part of their assignment. The "praise, prompt, and leave" method should not take more than thirty seconds per student. This allows you to see as many students as possible and it gives your students the necessary feedback they need for successful learning. It also helps you avoid getting overly involved with one student, forsaking the others.

If you have difficulties keeping students on task, first analyze the situation to determine exactly what activity or what teaching behavior is causing the off-task behavior. Steere has identified some questions to help you identify off-task behavior that could be damaging the climate you want to establish and maintain. A peer coach might be helpful for collecting the data needed to answer some of these questions.

How many minutes are spent each day:

- taking roll, collecting money, and attending to other homeroom activities?
- locating, distributing, and collecting materials?
- cleaning up, standing in line, going to the restroom or water?
- reviewing management rules and giving nonacademic directions?
- reprimanding students, thereby causing other students to be disturbed and pulled off task?
- by students being unengaged while waiting for the teacher?
- during which the staff members interfere with children's assigned tasks (examples: engaging in irrelevant talk, giving additional directions, having visitors, announcement of PA, being overemotional and loud in correcting behavior?
- with one (or a few) students while others need assistance?
- during which the teacher is unavailable to assist students (examples: speaking to a visitor, handling emergencies, and being tied up with one group)?
- on activities with marginal or little value to the instructional objectives?
- on lengthy student recitations before the teacher regains "leadership"?
- exceeding the time allotted for recess and lunch?
- allowing pupils to get drinks and go to the restroom during instructional time?
- when students are out of the room, during a lesson, for the convenience of scheduling remedial instruction?

(Reprinted by permission of the State University of New York Press, from *Becoming an Effective Classroom Manager: A Resource for Teachers* by Bob F. Steere, ©1988, State University of New York. All rights reserved.)

5.23 Which strategies do you plan to use to keep your students on task?

Classroom Procedures. Efficient and effective classroom procedures set up ahead of time positively affect the climate of your classroom. Introduce them throughout the first week of school as needed. Teach, model, role play (especially with younger children), and review them as often as necessary (perhaps everyday for younger children) for the first few weeks of school. Also remember that many children, especially younger ones, take your words literally. Therefore, if you want your students to stop doing something, say "stop" and not "cut it out." Doing all of these things helps ensure that students know what to do and when to do it. This increases industriousness and reduces the opportunities for discipline problems. Use the next set of questions to help you identify which classroom procedures are needed.

5.24 What are your classroom procedures for the following daily routines:

    a. waiting for class to officially begin?

    b. taking attendance?

    c. arriving late?

    d. obtaining transportation changes, especially for younger students, to help ensure your students get home safely?

    e. taking lunch count?

    f. recess (if applicable):

        i.   How long is it?

        ii.   Is it the same time everyday?

        iii. Where does it take place (playground, classroom, or gymnasium)? Does this change for different weather conditions?

        iv. What kinds of activities are allowed during indoor recess? Are they whole group activities or are they individualized free play time activities?

        v.   What are the rules for any games your students might play?

    g. snack time (if applicable):

        i.   What time does it take place?

        ii.   What are the rules during snack time?

        iii. Who provides the snacks?

    h. transitions between any two activities? entering and leaving the classroom?

    i. class meetings?

    j. dismissing after class officially ends?

5.25 What are your classroom procedures for the following classroom operations:

    a. getting your students' attention when you need it?

    b. using the lavatories and water fountains found inside and outside the classroom?

    c. eating food and drinking beverages in class?

d. sharing materials and supplies?

e. obtaining supplies during class time (such as obtaining pencils, pens, paper, glue, scissors, books, and so forth)?

f. touching, borrowing things from the teacher's desk and elsewhere in the room?

g. using any math manipulatives or science apparatus?

h. using any type of A/V equipment, including computers?

i. borrowing classroom library books?

j. returning school library books during a time other than the designated classroom library time or in between classes?

k. sharpening pencils?

    i. when and how to use the sharpener

    ii. what can and cannot be sharpened in the classroom sharpener

---

A True Story If you have ever taught young children, you know never to take anything for granted! I'll never forget the day my classroom's pencil sharpener jammed. I opened it and found crayon shavings and evidence of other things that should not have been placed in the sharpener. I also had many other oversights with other basic tools such as scissors, staplers, glue, paper clips, rubber bands, stapler removers, three-ring binders, and others. I learned my lesson—to teach young children (and older ones if they need it) how to properly use common office supplies and tools (and to keep a working spare electric pencil sharpener in the closet). Do not leave it to chance if you want to prevent stress!

---

l. cleaning up after themselves?

m. keeping their desks or workspaces and classroom neat and clean?

n. working classroom jobs?

o. handling classroom lost and found items?

p. handling disagreements or problems that arise in class (for example, if a student refuses to do work or refused to remove herself from the group)?

q. using a time-out area in the classroom?

r. giving feedback about the classroom (for example, using a classroom suggestion box)?

5.26 What are your classroom procedures for the following instructional events:

a. asking a question and joining class discussions?

b. telling you that they cannot see or hear you?

c. passing out and collecting:

    i. paper?

        ii.   textbooks?

        iii.   other items or supplies?

   d. evaluating each other's work (such as when students switch papers to check each other's work)?

   e. working in groups, such as reading groups, lab groups, and project groups?

   f. coming to a small group—what to bring, what to do while waiting for the group to start, and so forth?

5.27 What are your classroom procedures for working independently, such as:

   a. asking for help?

   b. talking during seatwork?

   c. finishing an in class assignment before their classmates?

   d. obtaining extra time to finish an in class assignment?

   e. leaving their seats—when is it allowed?

   f. sitting on the floor—where, when, how is it okay to sit?

   g. interrupting you when you are working with another student or a small group of students?

5.28 What are your classroom procedures for the following infrequent classroom events:

   a. interruptions by the intercom, visits from an unexpected guest or messenger?

   b. buying lunch when a student forgets her lunch or lunch money?

   c. borrowing P.E. equipment from the gymnasium for recess?

5.29 What are your procedures for written assignments with respect to:

   d. headings on papers?

   e. kinds of paper to be used?

   f. kinds of writing tools, such as pen or pencil, to be used?

5.30 What are your procedures for the following types of paperwork:

   a. homework?

        i.   How often is it assigned?

        ii.   Is it to be done in pen or pencil?

   b. weekly folders that go home?

   c. finding out and making up missed classwork, including tests, after returning from an absence?

   d. tests:

        i.   Are parents be expected to sign tests?

        ii.   Are students allowed to keep tests at home or do they return them to you?

iii. Are students asked to keep track of their own grades to help them keep tabs on what their final grade will be?

5.31 What are your classroom procedures for handing in

    a. homework?

    b. notes from home, including signed permission slips, tests, and report cards?

    c. completed in-class assignments?

5.32 What is your procedure for storing classwork that isn't completed in the allotted time?

5.33 Do any of the above procedures need to be written down and posted in the classroom?

5.34 Are all of the above procedures supportive of all of the expectations of you and of your class?

Classroom Rules. Most effective teachers have expectations for behavior that is understood by all of their students, whether or not they are written and posted on the wall. Rules stated positively help to define how you and your students *should* behave. The rules should be clear about behaviors that are okay some of the time, such as talking, and which are never okay, such as hitting. There should only be a few rules. Two to seven rules should be enough. They should be reasonable, necessary, observable, and reinforceable. Words that are difficult to understand for children, such as "respect" and "responsible," should be clearly explained. Consequences (positive and negative) should also be included. Consequences should be logical and reasonable. They should be related to the offense and should be respectful to the perpetrator. Remember, if you choose the right behaviors to emphasize, it helps you prevent problems that could lead to stress. So choose your rules carefully.

Your classsroom rules communicate your "discipline plan." It needs to be consistent with your school's overall discipline philosophy, appropriate for the age of your students, and flexible for adapting to individual differences The plan needs to provide students with their most basic needs of safety, belonging, and security. It also needs to be easy to administer and easy to communicate to both students, parents, and administrators.

Some teachers wish to create the classroom rules with their students. If you would like to do this, use questions like, "Why do we have rules?" and "What rules do you think we need in our classroom?" These questions help begin the conversation. Some teachers create contracts or classroom constitutions with their students. These are all fine. You can determine which strategy is right for you and your students. However, regardless of which strategy you use, you should identify ahead of time the rules you believe benefit your entire class. This ensures that these important rules are included in your final list and not accidentally overlooked.

After the rules are established, they need to be taught and reviewed as often as possible. Many teachers discuss them daily. They also role play situations where the rules are demonstrated until they become a part of the classroom culture. You know that this has happened when students are following the rules without having to be reminded of them.

The rules also need to be shared with parents. Parents, too, need an understanding of the classroom's expectations for behavior. You can include them in your Classroom Handbook or you can send a note home with a tear-off response slip that parents and students must sign to acknowledge that they are aware of your classroom rules and will support them.

Throughout the day, you might have to prompt your students to follow the rules. You can do this by sharing your expectations of how they should behave during a particular activity. You can also praise students who are following the rules by identifying the specific behavior you want others to follow. For example, thank a student for turning to page 10 so that you are also repeating the directions for another student who needs the prompt for the expected behavior. Lastly, if none of these work, you can issue a warning. If the student still chooses to break the rules, follow it with a consequence. Remember, the consequence must be appropriate for the offense.

A True Story I taught as a substitute teacher for one full year. During that time, I learned that it was imperative to state and explain my classroom rules within moments of arriving to my assigned class. Today, I still have the same two classroom rules: "respect others" and "do what you are supposed to be doing." I explain to my students that "respect" means to never, in any way, hurt another person. This includes making fun of another person, even if the person is not present. To explain the second rule, I first give examples. One example I use is to tell them that if they are supposed to be working with another student on an assignment, they should be working together and talking (I always see a slight surprise on their faces when I use this example). I go on to tell them that it is normal to not always know what they are supposed to be doing, however, it is not okay to take that opportunity to do something inappropriate to try to hide the fact that they do not know what is going on. I share that this is something that happens to everyone all the time, including to me. With deep sincerity, I add that it is not a problem and I encourage them to simply raise their hands and ask me for the information again. As a result, I have never had major discipline problems. In fact, I had so few problems as a substitute teacher that I was consistently called to substitute the more "difficult" classes. I will never forget the day I was a few minutes late to one such class and they told me that the students were upset that I had not yet arrived! For me, this was a testament to the power of simple, clear, reasonable rules and empathetic leadership.

5.35 Classroom rules:

    a. Keeping in mind the school rules, which behaviors are acceptable and unacceptable?

    b. What rules, if any, are needed to maintain appropriate behaviors?

c. What are positive consequences (rewards) and negative consequences for following or breaking the rules, respectively?

d. How and when do you plan to share these rules with your students? parents?

e. Do they support the expectations of you and of your class?

f. Should you post any of these rules to avoid confusion or forgetfulness?

Integrating New Students. Many of the things listed above are established during the first few days and weeks of school. What happens if a new student arrives in mid-December? New students might arrive at any time during the school year. The students need to become acclimated into your classroom. You want this to occur as smoothly and as quickly as possible to avoid detracting from the healthy classroom climate you have created. One way to do this is to buddy the new student with one of your more trustworthy students. Another way might be to create a "new student kit" which includes a classroom handbook and other things your student (and her parents) need in order to be successful in your class. Determine how you can successfully integrate new students so that when it happens you can just refer to your notes and not have to worry about how to handle it.

A True Story. I had a half dozen new students one year. I had not anticipated it, nor did I usually have much warning. In fact, I remember one student showing up at my door with the school secretary around ten o'clock in the morning. There was absolutely no warning and no prep time. As a result, I had to think on my feet and quickly figure out a way to welcome the child and to successfully integrate her into our class. If I had a plan in advance, it would have prevented a lot of stress.

5.36 New students during the school year:

a. How can you acclimate a new student to your classes, both socially and academically?

b. How can you acclimate a new student to your classroom's rules and procedures?

c. What items, such as book and supplies, do you need to make sure are provided to this student?

d. What kinds of information do you need in order to make an assessment of his achievement to date? Are the same kinds of information be needed as the year progresses?

Relationships with Parents

Your classroom's climate is also affected by your relationships with those outside of your class, such as your students' parents. Your relationships with your students' parents can make or break your career without you ever realizing it. Although this is not what you usually focus on, these relationships must be established and nurtured, just like the relationships with your students. Some of these relationships can be the most difficult challenges you face as a teacher, especially if you live in the community and plan on staying there.

To be successful, first establish rapport between your class and your students' parents with several positive interactions. After the rapport is established, maintain it with favorable opinions and images of your classroom. Basically, this boils down to a proactive public relations program.

The Beginning of the School Year. There are things that you can do ahead of time to help insure that you and your students' parents get off on the right foot. You need to think of yourself as a public relations manager whose task it is to make parents feel confident about you and about what is going on in your classroom. This is not an easy task. The following are some suggestions.

- Before school opens, send a letter to your students and their parents introducing yourself and welcoming them back to school.
- Before school opens, host your own "open house" if your school does not have a meet-the-teacher day, inviting both your students and their parents to meet you and to become familiar with the school and the classroom.
- Provide parents with weekly newsletters highlighting students' accomplishments.
- After the first two weeks of school, do some type of public relations activity at this opportune time of the school year, such as a telephone call or a postcard to each student and their parents telling them the good things the student is doing.
- Plan a parent tea or student presentation for parents within the first six weeks of school to show off your students' accomplishments.

Notice that many of the suggestions are things that should be done at the beginning of the school year. This is important because parent involvement and enthusiasm runs higher at the beginning of the school year than at any other time. Take advantage of this. Use the excitement and hype to your advantage by planning as many of these things at the beginning of the school year as possible.

5.37 What are the different things that you can use to promote a positive image of you and your students?

Open House or Back to School Night: These events are usually organized at a school level and are great opportunities to put your public relations plan in high gear. The following are some suggestions for making these events a success.

- If possible, send home a questionnaire before the event asking parents what they are interested in hearing and seeing.
- Display your students' best work proudly and neatly both inside and outside your classroom.
- Provide refreshments if the school does not.
- Provide nametags with space for both their name and their child's name.
- Make the classroom neat, clean, and inviting.
- Dress neat, clean, and professional.
- Provide sign up sheets for parent volunteers (if applicable).
- Make it clear that no personal problems will be discussed, but they can sign up to schedule a conference with you at a later time.
- Take the time to reiterate your expectations for their children's behavior and for homework.
- Explain the goals and objectives of the class and the major units of work that are covered.

- Explain how grades are determined.
- Allow time for parents to ask questions.
- Explain your procedure for parents to voice concerns and how you plan to handle the concerns.

5.38   What things can you do to make Open House or Back to School Night a success?

Involving Parents. Getting parents involved in the classroom is another way to promote the good things that are happening in your classroom. Invite them to participate in organized, effective educational activities with their children. Parents are invaluable resources for you and your students. Use a parent survey (also discussed in *Step 3: Know Your Resources*) the first few days of school to find out the interests, hobbies, and skills they want to share with you and your students. Parents also can be tutors, assistants, and clerical help for you and your class.

With many options available, you must first decide how you want to integrate parents into your classroom. Think this through *very* carefully. If you do not organize this well, you could be setting yourself up for some bad publicity. Remember, parents talk to one another. If they are present in your classroom and something goes terribly wrong, many more people will hear about it. On the other hand, if the event goes very smoothly and it is something where your students are successful, the parent will probably gain more confidence in you and your class. This situation can be a wonderful source of positive publicity. Therefore, careful planning is imperative.

5.39   In what ways do you want parents involved in your classroom?

After you figure out how you want parents involved, you need to figure out how to recruit them. One way is just to ask for parents help and involvement on an as needed basis. Another way is to set up a group of parent volunteers ahead of time, to establish a "classroom parents committee."

If you plan to have "classroom parents," it is imperative that you decide how you to organize your parents and how often you want them in the classroom during the instructional day. Determine this before the first day of school. One teacher limits parent volunteers to one time each during the first month of school in order to see how each parent works out. She then increases time as needed during the year. By starting out in this way, she is able to see how each parent works with the children, what are each parent's attitude and intentions, and how the children react to the parent. If it is not in her or her students' best interest to have a certain parent working in the classroom, this set up makes it easier for her to reduce that parent's time in the classroom. However you choose to involve parent volunteers, be prepared to explain it. Have your ideas set before the first day of school because you might have some parents asking you about this even before school opens!

A True Story One year before school even began, students and parents dropped by my classroom to meet me. Many of these parents expressed their interest in helping out during the school day. Although I did tell them briefly how I planned to involve parents in my class, I did not have a sign up sheet for specific activities. This was a missed opportunity to get more help for my students. Therefore, plan well in advance of the first day of school how you will involve parents, and be prepared with specifics when parents express their interest.

Your "classroom parents committee" needs just as much structure as your students. Establish procedures for the committee. Decide which parent will chair it and define the different roles of committee members. Identify tasks or events in which they will be involved and how they will be involved. Keep an open mind and get input from the parents, but do not leave the final decision making up to them—if you do, you might lose control over this precious resource, and your stress level will rise. Do not let this happen. Organize your classroom parents ahead of time as carefully as you organize your classroom. It pays huge dividends later.

5.40 Classroom Parents Committee:

    a. How do you organize your classroom parents?

    b. How do you ask for classroom parent volunteers?

        i. Do you post it in your weekly newsletter, send a note/memo to parents, use telephone calls, and/or put out a sign up sheet during Back to School Night or other time?

        ii. Do you state that "no experience is required" or that they need particular skills?

    c. How do you decide who chairs the committee, if anyone?

    d. What is each individual's role on the committee?

    e. What tasks or events will they work on?

    f. How often do you meet with the committee?

    g. How often do you want parents to be involved in your classroom during the instructional day?

    h. What procedures are needed to help keep the committee running smoothly?

5.41 For those parents who have not volunteered to be "classroom parents":

    a. How can you involve them in your class?

    b. How can you let them know you would like them involved in a particular activity or event?

    c. How can you use the classroom parents committee to help get other parents involved?

Working With Parents. When working with parents, remember to always treat them as very important partners in your students' education. Treat them with respect. Be professional. You are the teacher, not their buddy or their enemy. Yet, you are on the same side, working together for their children. Practice good communication skills such as listening carefully and listening more than speaking. Use tact, empathy, kindness, and consideration. When speaking, avoid educational jargon and use a tone that makes the parent feel comfortable with you and confident in you and your skills.

Parent-Teacher Conferences. For required parent-teacher conferences, you might want to send home a positive letter inviting the parents and asking them to check off the top three times they are available to meet with you. Whether or not the conference is required, include a questionnaire when you write back to confirm the appointment. The questionnaire should ask questions about what they feel are their child's strengths and weaknesses, how they can help their child at home, and any questions they might have for you. If the parent called the meeting, it is imperative that you find out in advance exactly what they want to discuss. If it is a complaint, perhaps taping the meeting or inviting witnesses, such as your principal or other staff members, might be necessary.

The following questions can help you to examine possible teacher behaviors that can help to establish and nurture your relationships with parents when meeting with them. Appendix E has some parent-teacher conference tips you might want to consider.

5.42 What kinds of things can you do to improve the chances of a successful parent-teacher conference?

    a. What does your conference invitation say?

    b. What questions can you include on your questionnaire?

    c. How can you schedule your conferences so that you do not have too many in a row?

    d. Are students allowed to attend the conference? Are their siblings also allowed?

Parents Role with Homework. Parents need to understand their role in their child's homework. They need to know how much assistance they should be giving their child. Remember to take into consideration all of the expectations about homework discussed in Chapter 3. Make your expectations clear to them in your Classroom Handbook or in a letter or newsletter to parents on the first day of school.

Homework is a way to teach students about responsibility. It should also be used to practice skills that have already been taught, been practiced under your supervision, and been understood. Homework assignments should ensure a high level of success, minimizing the opportunity for frustration on both the students' and the parents' part. Before students go home, they should understand exactly what is expected in the assignment.

5.43 What is the goal of homework?

5.44 What do you expect to be parents' role in homework?

5.45 How can you communicate this expectation?

Showing Parents That Their Children Are Special to You. Another way to improve your relationship with parents is to make sure that you show them that their children are special to you. Some parents are especially concerned about their child being recognized. A student recognition plan is one way to accomplish this. Even if one is not required, establish one in your classroom. Teachers often use "Student of the Week," show-and-tell, and other such programs to highlight students and their accomplishments. See what your colleagues are using. To get the most out of this activity, choose one that you feel is worthwhile, is developmentally appropriate, and helps students achieve some of the curriculum goals.

5.46 Do you have a student recognition program in your class?

    a. Which one is worthwhile, is developmentally appropriate, and helps students achieve some of the curriculum goals at the same time?

    b. How is it structured?

Another way to show parents that you believe their children are special is to celebrate their children's birthdays. This makes your students feel special and it allows parents to get involved in the celebration. Some teachers try to schedule the day or week when a student participates in a student recognition program, such as "Student of the Week," with the child's birthday. This is very efficient and does not let a student's birthday dampen anyone else's special week. To simplify matters, some teachers schedule one birthday party per month. Whatever you decide, make sure what you do follows school policy.

5.47 Birthdays:

    a. What do you want to do to celebrate a student's birthday (if their family's religious beliefs permit celebrating birthdays)?

    b. When and how do you want to celebrate birthdays that fall over weekends and vacations?

    c. How do you want to involve parents in the celebration?

Relationships with Whom You Work

Colleagues, administrators, and other staff members are part of your support network, so nurture these relationships as you would any other. Act professionally and assertively. Be considerate of others' feelings and respect their experience and opinions. Brainstorm ways in which you can strengthen these relationships.

5.48 What things can you do to build and support the relationships with your:

    a. colleagues

    b. administrators

    c. other school staff

    d. central office personnel

Physical Environments

As your primary environment, the classroom itself plays a major role in your classroom climate. Stress decreases when your classroom environment is organized, interesting, and clean. To prevent teacher stress, you must learn to manage your classroom's physical environment effectively and efficiently. This is very important because this is an area in which most of you have a considerable amount of control. The classroom environment consists of your classroom's floor plan (including furniture and storage areas) and decor (including walls, bulletin boards, and accessories).

Floor Plan

Your classroom's floor plan needs to accommodate several things in order to be effective for preventing potential stressors. The floor plan needs to optimize the use of the space while providing for the free movement of people within the classroom.

To accomplish this, take into account the traffic pattern in your classroom. Take note of high traffic areas such as the doors, the cubbies, and the storage areas. Other high traffic areas include the classroom's sink, bathroom, and water fountain. To promote safety and to prevent your students from getting in one another's way, these areas need to remain free of any physical obstacles.

There are several other things you need to consider when designing your floor plan. If you plan to work with your students in small groups or in stationary learning centers, you need to create a floor plan that accommodates these separate areas. These areas should not be totally hidden from the rest of the room. You need to be able to see everyone in your room from all vantage points at all times. You also need to make room to allow assistants and volunteers to work with your students during class time. If you teach younger children, you might also want a large floor area where your students can gather when you read a story to them. Regardless of your students' age, you might also want to set aside some quiet caddies in your room. Remember to also take note of the location of the intercom button or telephone, light switches, heating and cooling controls, and computer and telephone jacks before deciding on your floor plan.

You can place your students' desks or tables in a variety of different ways. Different arrangements are better than others at helping you achieve your goals. Experiment. Most schools do not bolt their desks down anymore, so if one arrangement doesn't work out, do not be afraid to change it. Visit your colleagues' classrooms to get ideas.

Whichever way you decide to arrange the desks or tables, sit at every seat. While imagining all of the seats filled, make sure that every one of your students has a clear view of you from where ever you lecture. Remember you must also make sure that you are able to see everyone from any vantage point in the room. Also, if you plan to rearrange your students' desks for different activities, remember to teach your students how to move furniture safely and practice this transition until your class can do it safely and smoothly.

Use the following questions for assessing your floor plan.

5.49 Can every student see the chalkboard and you from where you teach?

5.50 Can every student see the pull-down screen (used for an overhead projector and a film projector), television, and any other visual aid you plan to use?

5.51 Can you see everyone from anywhere in the classroom?

5.52 Are high traffic areas clear?

5.53 If you have learning centers, are quiet ones away from noisy ones?

5.54 Does the floor plan support your educational objectives, your teaching style, and your students' learning styles?

5.55 Are seats and cubbies assigned?

5.56 Are nametags made for each student's desk and cubby so they know what space belongs to them?

Where you place your desk and your assistant's desk (if you have an assistant) is another variable. You need to decide how much time you spend at your desk during the school day and where you want it in relation to the door of your classroom. Again, if you are unsure as to where to place it, ask your colleagues where they place them and why. You might find it interesting to hear their reasons.

A True Story When I taught first grade, I had many parents bring their children to class each morning. At the beginning of the year, I had my desk in the far corner of the room away from the door. As a result, parents would come in and end up staying a long time—looking at all of my bulletin boards and talking with their child's classmates. This became a huge distraction for most of my students. Other teachers had similar problems and solved it by placing their desk closer to the door. I placed my desk near the door, resembling a receptionist's desk. I also tried to spend more time at my desk during arrival time. It worked beautifully, and as a bonus, it made it easier to greet my students as they entered the door and to establish a positive classroom climate for the day!

Storage Areas

Other things you must consider are where you plan to store materials that your students need access to during the school day, such as personal belongings, books, glue, scissors, and math manipulatives. Keep them easy to get to so that your students can be self-sufficient.

5.57 Is there a place in the room for your students personal belongings, such as coat, bookbag, and books?

5.58 Where can you store materials that your students need? that you need?

Storage areas can get messy. Motivate your students to keep their desks, cubbies, and other personal workspaces neat and clean by giving them the time to straighten up the areas and the sponges to wipe them down, if necessary.

Classroom Decor

Your classroom decor compliments your floor plan. It includes your window and wall treatments, plants, odors, and accessories. To prevent stress, the room needs to feel soothing, comfortable, and inviting. Colors used to decorate the room, including bulletin boards, should be in soothing colors, such as blues and greens. Pale pink, peach, and other pastels are also good choices. Avoid bright red and orange. Window curtains, even very inexpensive ones, plants, and fresh cut flowers add an inviting touch to any room. They help to soften the lines and surfaces of chalkboards, windows, bookshelves, and tables. Air fresheners and opening the windows to change the air in the classroom (if permitted) help the room smell fresh and pleasant.

Bulletin Boards

Bulletin boards can have multiple purposes. They can be entertaining, display areas, or interactive. Interactive bulletin boards invite the student to do an activity. Decide how you want to use each of your bulletin boards. They can send powerful messages to anyone who visits your room about what kind of teacher you are and how your classroom is run.

Some teachers say to fill up the walls with bulletin boards, posters, and other things to make the room stimulating. Others say to keep it simple yet attractive. They believe the environment should not distract the students. Because there are good arguments for both sides, you must decide for yourself. How? Again, experiment. Try each way for a few weeks and see how your students respond. If the stimulating walls help you and your students achieve your goals, keep it. If they make it more difficult to keep your students on task, then go with the simple look. Every class is different. Every teacher is different. Find out what works for you and your students. The decor that helps your students work well helps you prevent stress.

5.59 How do you plan to decorate your classroom to make it conducive to learning?

5.60 How do you plan to use your bulletin boards to support and enhance your goals?

5.61 Does your decor (especially curtains and bulletin board background paper) violate any fire codes?

If you do not have your own classroom and must share other teachers' classrooms throughout the day, identify how much input you have in your classrooms' environments. Influence it as much as you can. An option might be to rearrange the desks while you conduct class and to put them back when you are through. Be creative!

Time

If time is not managed properly, the classroom's climate is impacted. You and your students can feel rushed. A lack of time becomes a stressor. As noted in an earlier chapter, a lack of time is often cited as the number one stressor by teachers. Therefore, this topic needs extra attention. To prevent stress, you must effectively manage both instructional time and planning time.

Instructional Time. Instructional time deals with managing the pace of the lesson and the flow of activities. The pace of the lesson has to be developmentally appropriate for your students. A steady, comfortable pace is best.

Be careful not to dwell upon a certain part of a lesson. Dwelling occurs when the teacher spends too much time on directions or on information that is irrelevant to the topic or goal. Do not fragment the lesson, either. A lesson is fragmented when it is broken up into too many unnecessary steps.

You also need to pay attention to the flow of your activities. A variety of activities is usually preferred. Transitions between them need to be short and organized. A poor transition can negatively impact your climate because it provides students with the opportunity to engage in inappropriate behavior.

Transitions occur both inside and outside your classroom. They occur within and between lessons, coming to and leaving from your classroom, and other movements between activities in which your entire class participates outside of your classroom (such as going to the restrooms or to the cafeteria). To help you with your transitions, first identify all of the possible transitions you could have in a given day, both inside and outside your classroom. Second, choreograph the transitions to be short and organized. Third, practice them yourself. Finally, practice them with your students.

If you still tend to "lose" your students during transitions, get help. Ask your colleagues about how they handle their transitions. Observe other teachers. Ask veteran teachers to observe you and your class and to offer suggestions. There are also books and chapters of books that deal with this very thing. Again, if you need help on transitions, seek help. There is plenty available.

A True Story When I began teaching, I had horrible transitions. A few of my colleagues and administrators observed me and my class and offered suggestions. Many suggestions focused on allowing a few children to transition at one time. One example was to allow only about five or six students to line up at the door at one time. These simple strategies became my saving grace that year.

Finally, the length of the lessons need to correspond to your class' attention span. Therefore, the general rule is to keep the length of lessons shorter for younger children and for children with learning difficulties.

5.62 Knowing the age and development of your students:

a. what should the pace of your lesson be?

b. what flow of activities would be more appropriate for them?

c. what kinds of games or ways can you use to help your students transition quickly and smoothly between lessons?

Planning Time. You must manage your planning time very effectively and very efficiently in order to prevent stress. Planning time consists of the time during the school day that is allocated for your personal use, as well as the personal time that you give up for this task. Earlier in this chapter, you identified the time that could be used for planning. Now look at maximizing the use of that time.

A general strategy for better managing your time consists of five steps.

- **Analyze**
  Record how you spend your time. Figure out on which thing or things you spend too much time.

- **Set goals**
  Identify the things that you want to accomplish and by what time.

- **Prioritize**
  Decide which goals must be achieved first. Group similar tasks together to save even more time.

- **Delegate**
  Farm out some of the work that someone else can do. Delegate tasks to your students, students' parents, teacher assistants, volunteers, and your own family members, if they don't mind.

- **Plan**
  Create an action plan that describes how you can achieve the goals.

The action plan can include several of the following time management tips to help maximize your efficiency. There have been several books written about time management over the last couple of decades. Check them out for time saving ideas. The following are some general time management tips:

- Prioritize activities.

- Avoid extra work by learning how to say "no."

- Structure time by allotting a reasonable amount of time for a task and moving on to something else when the time is over.

- Take short breaks.

- Pace yourself.

- Handle each piece of paper once (either act on it immediately, file it for future action, refer it to someone else, or throw it out).

- Expect that you might not be done at the end of the day; there is always more to do.

- Do one thing at a time.

- Do not let others waste your time.

- Learn to delegate.

- Avoid perfectionism.
- Stay organized.

Ask your colleagues what they do to save time, and use your creativity to think of some other ways. The following are some time management tips specifically for teachers that perhaps you could also use.

- Create forms for recording information from meetings, observations of students, grades, and anecdotal notes.
- Create conference forms that include a place for you to record questions you need to ask and a place to record outcomes of the conversation.
- Prioritize students' assignments and which parts of them you will check (for example, the first and last problems on homework assignments).
- Check students' in class or homework assignments only on certain days of the week, and allow students to check their own or each others' work often.
- Keep folders or index cards with each child's emergency information handy.
- Use a spreadsheet program or other software application to record and average grades.

Ask yourself the following questions to help you identify your biggest time wasters and to put some plans in place to address them.

5.63 How do you spend your planning time? Do you spend too much time on certain tasks?

5.64 How can you structure your planning time and organize yourself so that you can accomplish as much as possible?

5.65 Which time management tips can you use to maximize your efficiency?

Schedules—Another Look

At the beginning of this chapter you allocated time for personal activities and outlined your teaching schedule. In this section, you put the details into your teaching schedule—the unit plans and climate plans you developed in the rest of this chapter.

Using the "Pacing Chart" in *7 Steps to Stress Free Teaching Plan Book* or a twelve month chart that is usually found in plan books, write in approximate timeframes for each of the units you decided to do.

5.66 Knowing the units you have chosen and the number and types of goals in each unit, does it appear you have enough time to cover all of the goals? Do some units have to be further combined or integrated?

Examine all of time you designated as planning time. Remember, you need to use this planning time to accomplish many tasks. The following are only some of the many things for which you need to use your planning time:

- developing unit plans and associated lesson plans
- designing and developing the things to establish, maintain, or improve your classroom climate (including decorating your classroom, developing procedures, writing newsletters, and making telephone calls) before and after the first day of school
- grading papers and recording grades
- completing paperwork required by your employer and school (including report cards)

With so many things to do, how can you allocate your planning time so that you can get everything done that you need to get done? The answer is to first prioritize your tasks. Ask yourself:

5.67 What must get done right away?

5.68 Can you delegate any of these tasks or parts of these tasks?

Mark a reasonable amount of time on your weekly plan book pages for each high priority task. As each day passes, keep re-evaluating your priorities, and make sure that you are scheduling enough time to complete them.

Once school is in session, your room is set up, procedures and rules are established, your classroom handbook is complete, and other one-time tasks are done. However, you still need to use your planning time to complete the day-to-day tasks listed above. To help you prevent stress, take control now by setting aside the planning time to do these routine tasks.

5.69 When can you:

    a. develop your resource units?

    b. correct papers?

    c. work on weekly newsletters to parents?

    d. open and respond to parents' notes and other mail?

To help you get the most out of your planning time, try to do your most difficult tasks during the planning time that coincides with your "best time" described in the beginning of this chapter. Also, do not over schedule every moment of your day. Things come up. Leave some breathing room for flexibility in your daily planning time.

Summary

In this chapter you created a plan to help you prevent stress. You also carved out the time you can use to execute your plan. The next step is to implement your plan and to analyze its effectiveness for helping you prevent stress.

Chapter 7

Step 6:

Implement and Assess the Plan

As you implement the plan that you have put in place in *Step 5: Create a Plan*, you have to assess if it meets the goals it was set up to achieve. The goals are those identified in *Step 4: Determine the Goals*, and the overall goal of this book, preventing stress.

Are You Achieving Your Goals?

As a teacher, you know that you must continually assess your students, whether you are engaged in a testing situation or not. It is the same with your plan. You need to be aware of your progress at all time.

To see if you are meeting your personal goals, determine whether or not you have actually taken the time to do the things you planned. Now decide whether or not you were able to accomplish everything you set out to do in the allotted time.

For checking your students' progress toward the curriculum goals and other goals you outlined for them, use formative and summative evaluations, assessment during your lessons and at the end of a unit, respectively. Use pre- and post-unit tests as another way to measure progress toward the goals.

There are a number of ways to check whether or not you are meeting your climate goals. To help you identify student behaviors that are detracting from your climate, keep a log of class behaviors for a week. Examine your log for patterns. Identify behaviors that are keeping you and your class from achieving your classroom climate goals. Also use the log to find clues to the causes of the inappropriate behavior. If you are still not sure what is detracting from the climate, ask a trusted colleague to observe you and your class in action. They might be able to point out possible causes.

If your classroom's climate is still not meeting your goals, take the following steps to identify and correct potential problems.

- **Your room arrangement.** Does is allow for smooth traffic flow? Are all students able to see you and the chalkboard? Can you see everyone from any point in the room?

- **Classroom management skills.** Is the room organized or is it chaotic? Are you able to get your students attention when you need it? Do you have a special signal to do this? Are your students aware of it and have you practiced it with them?

- **Classroom rules.** Are they effective? Do all of your students understand them? Do they need to be discussed, reviewed, or role played some more?

- **Classroom procedures.** Do they need to be reviewed? Are there procedures for all of the things that could potentially cause you and your students problems?

- **Inappropriate behavior.** Is inappropriate behavior being nipped in the bud?

- **Transitions.** Are transitions smooth and orderly?

- **Lesson plans.** Are your lessons developmentally appropriate for your students? Have you individualized instruction to accommodate different learning styles and learning needs in order to reduce opportunities for inappropriate behavior?

To determine whether or not your climate goals dealing with the relationships between your class and everyone else are being achieved, examine the feedback you are getting from parents, colleagues, and administrators. If their overall tone is negative, figure out why they do not think highly of you and of your class. Then, adjust your plan to address it. If their overall tone is positive, you are probably meeting your goals. Continue the bulk of what you are doing, adjust any of the activities that you think might still need tweaking, and eliminate those that do not affect your climate at all.

6.1   Are you achieving your goals identified in Step 4?

    a. personal

    b. student

    c. climate

6.2   If you are not achieving your goals,

    a. why not?

    b. which part of your plan needs adjusting?

Are You Preventing Stress?

Is your plan helping you prevent stress? The way to determine this is to again complete the stress inventory you did in Chapter 1. Doing this inventory again can help you identify whether or not you are still affected by the same stressors. It can also help you identify any new stressors in your life.

The list of questions needed to complete the inventory and another copy of the Stress Inventory are below for your convenience. Again, copy the inventory into your notebook and give yourself as many lines as you need.

The questions used to complete the inventory are the following:

- **Stressor**: What events cause you stress?

- **Who/What**: Who or what is involved in each stressful event? Is it a particular student, colleague, administrator, or parent? Is your own family involved? Are you the only one involved? Are your teaching materials, textbooks, computers, or other equipment involved? Write the name of the person or thing that is involved in each stressful event.

- **Where**: Where does each stressor occur? Does it occur at home, at school (such as the classroom, the teachers' lounge, the main office, the playground, and so forth), on the telephone, or some other place? Specify exactly where each one occurs.

- **Frequency**: How often does each one occur? Is it always, often, or seldom?

- **Amount of Control**: How much control do you *feel* you have over each event? Is it a high level of control, some control, or no control?

- **Coping Strategies**: How do you currently deal with each stressor? Do you get depressed, frustrated, or angry, or do you just laugh it off? Do you enlist the support of others? Specify exactly what you do in each event.

Stress Inventory

Stressor	Who/What	Where	Frequency	Amount of Control	Coping Strategies

Analyze the results of your inventory. Are you able to group your stressors in any way? Are there different stressors in your life now than when you first completed the "Stress Inventory"? Are there now fewer stressors related to your job? Compare your results with the results you obtained in Chapter 1.

6.3   Are the stressors the same as before, or are they different?

6.4   Are there more or fewer stressors in your life right now than when you first began this book?

If your plan has not reduced the number of stressors in your life, then something needs to be adjusted, but what? First, identify which stressors or groups of stressors are causing most of your stress.

6.5   Which stressors or groups of stressors are causing most of your stress?

Examine your goals and your plan with respect to your current stressors.

6.6   Do your goals or does your plan have something in place to address your current stressors?

If you answered "no" to this question, then you need to put something in place to address your stressors. By asking yourself empowering questions, like those found in *Step 1* through *Step 3*, you can identify what might be needed.

If you answered "yes" to this question, then you must figure out why your plan is not working. You must determine where the breakdown is occurring. Use the following questions to help you figure it out.

6.7   Are the goals you chose in *Step 4: Determine the Goals* appropriate for addressing the stressors? Does the plan achieve those goals without adding new stressors?

6.8   Does your plan contain activities that help you achieve your goals?
       a.   Are you following your plan?
       b.   Is the schedule comfortable, too tight, or too slow?

6.9   Does your plan take advantage of all the resources that are available to you?

If the breakdown is occurring because of inappropriate goals or an ineffective, inefficient plan, make necessary adjustments. Check to make sure your goals and your plan are in sync, and try again. If you are finding that your plan is not working because you are not implementing or following the plan properly, get motivated! If you do, you have so much to gain and so much pain to lose. Work your plan. It might not be easy, but the rewards are great!

Summary

After you know where you want to go and have a plan to get there, you must figure out if you are on the right path. If the plan is not working, try to figure out why, and then try something else. Make some plan adjustments and keep going. Never stop watching for progress. Analyze and evaluate your plan on a daily basis. Make this step a part of your everyday routine. Work it in like your breathing; do it unconsciously, yet always be aware of its importance.

Remember, as you go through this process, you are fine tuning your goals, your plan, and your skills to control events that might lead to stress. In essence, you are becoming a "stress preventer"!

Chapter 8

Step 7:

Reflect

Reflecting means examining your actions. Examine your actions by asking questions about them and about the beliefs behind them. This process needs to be a part of your life because it helps you evaluate your growth as a teacher and as a person.

Although this step is related to *Step 6: Implement and Assess the Plan*, it does play a different role. This step's role is to reflect on the entire stress prevention journey—to look at where you are today in comparison to where you started.

How Much Have You Grown?

Reflect upon your overall growth as a teacher. To identify areas of growth (or lack of them), evaluate your current teaching skills. This can be accomplished in several ways.

Others' Evaluations

One way to evaluate your teaching skills is to ask your principal or other supervisors to evaluate your teaching. In many schools this is a requirement, not an option. Regardless, they can be helpful. Another way is to ask a trusted colleague to observe you and to give you feedback.

Your students can be another source for evaluations, especially if your students are older. If you do ask your students to evaluate your teaching, make sure that it is done in writing. You can use a classroom suggestion box during the year, or you can ask your students to respond to the following questions about your class:

- What do you like or hate about this class?
- If there is one thing that you could change, what would it be?
- What are the most important classroom procedures? rules?
- What have you learned so far this year?

Your students' answers can be invaluable because they have a different perspective of your class than you do.

Your Self-Evaluation

You also need to do a self-evaluation. Take an honest look at your teaching skills. Using the "How Much Have You Grown?" checklist on page 123, rate yourself on where you were at the beginning of your current teaching assignment (for many, this equals the "beginning of the year") and where you are now. Use a score of 1 to 10, with 10 being the highest. Calculate an average for each column.

7.1 Is today's average higher or lower than your average at the beginning of the year (or when you first starting this teaching assignment)?

7.2 Are you pleased with your progress? Why or why not?

7.3 Can you identify areas of strength?

7.4 Can you identify areas of weakness?
   a. What goals can you put in place to improve these areas?
   b. What plans do you need to accomplish this goal?

You must also evaluate your growth as an individual. Use today and the day you started reading this book as points of reference. Use the following questions to help you get started in evaluating your personal growth.

7.5 How "stressed out" do you feel today compared to the day you began reading this book?

7.6 Are you feeling stronger and more in control?

7.7 Is your self-esteem higher?

7.8 Do you have hope for a better tomorrow?

How Much Have You Grown?

	Beginning of Year	[Today]
Class Control		
Varying Lesson Techniques		
Reaching all students		
Making lessons interesting		
Motivating [your] students		
Putting subject matter across		
Controlling [your] emotions		
Developing an esprit de corps		
Getting along with other teachers		
Cooperating with administrators		
Taking care of individual differences		
Identifying children with problems		
Writing effective lesson plans		
Creating effective tests and quizzes		
Correcting papers on time		
Keeping adequate records		
Dealings with parents		
Classroom routine		
Handling special duties		
Improving [your] knowledge of subject matter		
Final Average		

From Elbert M. Hoppenstedt, *A Teacher's Guide to Classroom Management,* © 1991. Courtesy of Charles C Thomas, Publisher, Ltd., Springfield, Illinois.

Whether or not you feel you have less stress today than the day you began reading this book, I would love to hear from you. I want to hear your success stories as well as your trials and tribulations. I want to know how these steps have helped you and if any step in particular made an impact in your life. Please contact me by writing to the publisher. Keep those letters coming! *I* grow by listening to you.

Changes for Next Time

Examine the successes and not-so-successful actions of your stress prevention journey. Are there things that you wish you had done differently? Identify what they are. Use the following questions to help you explore the things you can, and want, to do differently next time—for tomorrow or for the next school year.

7.9 Was the stress prevention journey to this day satisfying? difficult?

7.10 Was the pace of your journey steady? realistic? comfortable?

7.11 Do you want to keep the same goals, or do you want to change some of them?

7.12 Has your plan been simple to implement?

7.13 What mistakes do you want to avoid?

7.14 What could you do differently? What do you *want* to do differently?

Your Future

Now look to the future. "Where do you go from here?" Perhaps a better question might be, "Where do you *want* to go from here?" Ask yourself the following:

7.15 What kind of teacher and person do you want to be five years from now?

7.16 What do you need to do to become that teacher and person?

7.17 Can you apply what you have learned in this book to other areas of your life? How?

Remember, you can be as good a teacher, parent, friend, or person as you want to be. You are in control of your life.

Continually reflect on your actions and beliefs so that you can grow and reach your full potential. Never become complacent, for it will kill your motivation and your desire to become all that you can.

Believe that no matter what the stressor is, you have some control over it. Control over a stressor is key for preventing stress.

Finally, look forward to a better tomorrow and to a better you. Take heart. There *is* a light at the end of the tunnel.

Summary

This book has been a stress prevention journey. At the beginning, you looked at where you were and where you wanted to go. You created plans and implemented those plans. Finally, you reflected upon the success of your plans and upon your growth as a teacher and as a person. For the future, continue to reflect upon the stress prevention process you experienced and make any adjustments in your goals and in your plans to help you continue to prevent stress.

Peer Support Groups

This is the procedure outlined by Scaros for conducting peer support group meetings.

A.1 Form a support group of 4 - 6 peers that you can trust and that trust one another.

A.2 One person (the focus person) discusses a work related problem (challenge) that she is having.

A.3 The support group asks questions to clarify the problem and the focus person records it on the Challenge Sheet (an example is found on the next page).

A.4 The support group then brainstorms possible solutions to the problem. Without comments or questions, the focus person writes all of the suggestions on the Challenge Sheet.

A.5 The focus person then takes the opportunity to clarify any or all of the brainstormed suggestions.

A.6 The remainder of the time is used for helping the focus person decide what is the best action to take based upon the brainstormed suggestions and to record it in contract form on the Challenge Sheet.

A.7 Another meeting time for additional support is scheduled.

A new person then becomes the next focus person, and steps 2 through 7 are repeated.

Challenge Sheet

Date:

Challenge:

_____

_____

_____

Brainstormed Suggestions:

_____

_____

_____

_____

_____

_____

_____

_____

Agreement:

I, _____ will _____

_____

_____ by _____

[Focus Person's] Signature: _____

Support Persons:

_____

_____

_____

Planning Celebrations

To prevent potentially stressful celebrations, use these questions when planning a classroom celebration or party.

B.1   When and where will the celebration take place?

B.2   Will there be food and beverages?
    a.   What kinds?
    b.   Who is in charge of bringing or buying it?
    c.   How is it served? by whom?
    d.   What serving utensils and containers are needed? Who supplies them?
    e.   Who supplies the plates, cups, napkins, and utensils?
    f.   How much does it cost and how is it paid for?

B.3   Will there be decorations?
    a.   Who buys or makes them?
    b.   Who does the decorating?

B.4   Who cleans up afterwards? What cleaning supplies are needed?

B.5   Will there be music?

    a.   What kind?

    b.   Who can bring the stereo, radio, other necessary equipment?

    c.   Who can bring audiocassettes or CDs?

    d.   Will the noise disturb other people?

    e.   Who is in charge of choosing and changing the music?

    f.   Who regulates the volume?

B.6   Will there be games?

    a.   Who can bring the games?

    b.   Who is in charge of participants?

    c.   Are there prizes? Where do they come from?

    d.   Who decides the winners?

B.7   Has the necessary permission been given?

Class Trips

There are four major stages for taking class trips. The first stage includes planning an educational purpose for the trip and selecting where you and your class will go. Second is organizing the trip. Third is taking the class trip. The last stage is evaluating the trip.

The first stage is done when you create your unit plans (done in *Step 5* of this book). The place you plan on attending should have some relevance to your curriculum. Also ask the following:

C.1 How many trips are you allowed to take?

C.2 Where are you allowed to go?

C.3 How do the places chosen support your curriculum?

The second stage is where all of the "leg work" takes place. You need to familiarize yourself with the site, including any overnight accommodations, and any school procedures for taking a class trip. You need to check the following:

C.4 What is the procedure to get

    a. permission (from school and from parents)?

    b. transportation? Which types of transportation are allowed?

      c. chaperones?

      d. funding for students', teachers', and chaperones' admission and transportation costs (including any tips for the driver, if applicable)?

C.5 Is a check or cash used to pay for

      a. admission?

      b. transportation?

C.6 How far in advance of the actual trip are you required to have it planned?

C.7 Do you need reservations? Are large groups only admitted on certain days or during certain hours?

C.8 What and where are the site's facilities for:

      a. restrooms?

      b. eating?

      c. overnight accommodations (if applicable)?

          i. Is round the clock security provided or must you provide your own?

         ii. Is an effort made to keep your rooms together?

      d. souvenirs?

C.9 What are the rules regarding sleeping arrangements if overnight accommodations are necessary?

C.10 Chaperones:

      a. What is the maximum chaperone to student ratio that is allowed?

      b. Besides parents, can other teachers who work with your students be asked to chaperone?

      c. Are chaperones allowed to take the same transportation as the students?

      d. If parents must drive themselves, are they allowed to drive their own children to and from the destination? Are they allowed to drive other students?

      e. Are chaperones allowed to bring other children who are not a part of your class?

      f. Are chaperones allowed to take students directly home from the site or must students return to school first to sign out?

C.11 If the trip extends through the time for breakfast, for lunch, or for dinner,

    a. do students need to bring their own food and drink, or are they provided?

    b. If food and drink is provided, is there an additional cost?

    c. If you bring our own food and drink, do you need to provide coolers to prevent spoilage?

C.12 If you take a bus, what are the bus driver's rules and procedures with respect to seating arrangement, noise levels, eating food and beverages on the bus, and so forth?

After the trip is planned, both students and chaperones need to be made aware of several things. Use the following questions to help you identify them:

C.13 Do your students and chaperones know

    a. the educational purpose of this trip?

    b. what kind of things they should be looking for on the trip?

    c. what kind of follow up work they need to do when you return from the trip?

C.14 Do your students and chaperones understand

    a. what they should and should not

        i. wear?

        ii. bring?

    b. when money and permission slips are due?

    c. appropriate behavior

        i. at the site?

        ii. on the bus (or other transportation vehicle)?

    d. where they must sit on the bus or at the site (if applicable)?

    e. what they should do in case they get lost or hurt?

    f. when and where they need to meet the group?

On the day of the trip, use the following questions to help you with last minute concerns:

C.15 Have your students and chaperones been given necessary nametags, maps, instructions, and directions?

C.16 Have you packed extra band-aids, handi-wipes, paper towels, and trash bags?

C.17 Do you have emergency telephone numbers for all of your students?

After returning from the trip, you and your students should evaluate it. Different aspects of the trip must be looked at in order to make changes and improvements for next time. Use the following questions to help you pinpoint the things that you need to review.

C.18 Did your students gain the knowledge you hoped they would?

C.19 Did your students see how the trip related to their curriculum?

C.20 Were your students behaved at every aspect of the trip?

C.21 Was the site appropriate
    a. for your goals?
    b. in size and in accommodations?
    c. for the interest and level of your students?

C.22 Were the transportation arrangements provide adequate space and safety? Were they afford-able?

C.23 Was the length of the ride too long?

C.24 Were the chaperones on the trip adequately prepared for their assignments?

C.25 Were there any problems or complications that were not anticipated?

Substitute Teacher Kit

This is a checklist of different things a substitute teacher might need. Include them in your "substitute teacher kit"—the information and plans you provide for a substitute teacher.

D.1   Lists:

  a.   class rosters

  b.   names of students who are helpful and trustworthy

  c.   names of students who have behavior or academic difficulties

  d.   names of students who have behavior or academic contracts and an explanation of how the contracts work

  e.   names of students who need to take medication, when, and who is allowed to administer the medication

  f.   names of students that have existing health problems and emergency procedures to handle them

  g.   members of different reading, lab, or other groups you have in your class

  h.   assistants and volunteers, including the time they are available and their responsibilities

  i.   names and titles of staff members, including names of teachers next door, who can answer any questions during the day

  j.   transportation information for each student

D.2 Maps:

    a. school

    b. classroom seating charts

    c. cafeteria seating chart

    d. emergency escape routes and locations for your class during inclement weather

D.3 Schedules:

    a. daily class related activities, including, but not limited to:

        i. arrival and dismissal times

        ii. schedule of lessons and other classroom activities

        iii. lunch

        iv. recess

        v. special classes, such as Art, Music, etc. (also note day, time, and place)

    b. students' volunteer activities, such as office helpers, custodial helpers, and safety patrol helpers

    c. your extra duties (such as bus, lunch, etc.) and a description of associated responsibilities

    d. students' pull-out (your students leave your classroom to work with another teacher) or push-in (another teacher comes into your classroom to work with your students) activities, including resource, band, and others

D.4 Important school and classroom rules to insure a smooth day including, but not limited to:

    a. classroom management and discipline system

    b. when it is appropriate to send a student to the office and the procedure to follow when doing so

D.5 important school and classroom procedures to insure a smooth day, including, but not limited to:

    a. emergency (fire, severe weather, first aid, etc.)

    b. arrival and dismissal routines

    c. sign in and sign out procedures for students and teachers

    d. attendance procedures (including collecting absentee notes)

    e. hallway, restroom, and water fountain use

D.6   Plans:

    a.   lesson plans with all needed materials or the location of the plans and materials denoted in the plans

    b.   grade book, if necessary

    c.   extra activities in case students finish their work early or in case lesson plans do not go as planned

D.7   A substitute feedback form that includes sections to write:

    a.   the substitute teacher's name and home telephone number

    b.   a way to indicate which plans were completed

    c.   a list of names of absent students

    d.   any extra work that was done

    e.   any behavior problems

    f.   general notes and comments

Parent-Teacher Conferences

Here are some tips for a successful parent-teacher conference:

- Schedule breathing room before and after the conference.
- Make an outline of the points you want to cover.
- If other teachers will also attend the conference, hold a briefing before the conference to make sure everyone has the same information and is aware of the goals of the conference.
- Use a table and adult sized chairs, sit beside the parent (not across).
- Dress professionally.
- Be on time.
- Have a place to put coats and umbrellas.
- Have paper and pencil available for the parent to use.
- Sit where you can see a clock.
- Keep a chair outside your door for parents who are waiting for their turn.
- Select one or two goals for the conference.
- Be ready to discuss the students' academic level.
- Be able to interpret standardized test scores.

- Have all of the students work that you want to share and any notes you need ready.
- Share the work with the student prior to the conference, if possible.
- Use a firm handshake and their names as you welcome them inside your classroom.
- Begin on a positive note by pointing out students strengths.
- Present proof of student's growth; there should not be any surprises.
- Watch parents' body language and tone.
- Listen attentively.
- Be empathetic.
- Gather information about the child from the parents.
- Let parents talk and ask questions; if they disagree with what you are saying, hear them out and respond with, "I hear what you are saying. Let's work things out together."
- Present a fair, impartial, complete, and meaningful evaluation of the child.
- Use anecdotal data to provide examples of behavior instead of labeling a child as lazy, disobedient, and so forth.
- Keep the conversation focused on the student.
- Do not compare the student with others.
- Have resources handy to send home with the parent, such as telephone numbers of counseling services and tutors (if allowed); book lists; lists of activities to do at home; and homework tips.
- Identify ways you can work together to help the student.
- Determine a follow up schedule to inform parents about their child's progress.
- Do not make any promises that you might not be able to keep.
- Let them know how to set up another conference with you in the future.
- Keep the conference to about 20 minutes.
- End on a positive note.
- See the parent to the door and thank them for coming.
- Keep the conversation confidential.
- Send a follow up note summarizing key points of the conference.

Parent Survey

Here is a sample parent survey that you can use to gather information about your students' parents. The information collected can be used to help you effectively integrate parents into your classroom.

Name:
Address:
Daytime telephone:

Please circle the activities you are interested in doing for your child's class:
        informal talks
        demonstrations
        sharing items from your home

If you are interested in doing an informal talk, please circle the general subject you would like to present and specify what the particular topic would be:
        job:
        hobby:
        travels:
        country of origin or of family's ancestors:
        other:

If you are interested in sharing any special talents by doing a demonstration, please circle the general topic and specify what the demonstration would be:

childcare:

crafts:

cooking:

dance:

drawing/painting:

exercise:

financial investing:

gardening:

hobbies:

music (voice or musical instrument):

pets:

other:

If you are interested in sharing any collections or items from your home, please specify:

videos, films, CDs (music), and so forth:

souvenirs, figurine collections, costumes, and so forth:

computer software or hardware:

other:

Professional Organizations

American Alliance for Health, Physical
Education, Recreation and Dance
1900 Association Drive
Reston, VA 22091
(703) 476-3400

American Association of Physics Teachers
1 Physics Ellipse
College Park, MD 20740
(301) 209-3300

American Council of the Teaching of Foreign
Languages
6 Executive Plaza
Yonkers, NY 10701
(914) 963-8830

American Federation of Teachers
555 New Jersey Avenue, NW
Washington, D.C. 20001
(202) 879-4400

American Library Association
50 E. Huron Street
Chicago, IL 60611
(312) 944-6780

American School Counselor Association
801 North Fairfax Street, Suite. 310
Alexandria, VA 22314
(703) 683-2722

American Speech-Language-Hearing
Association
10801 Rockville Pike
Rockville, MD 20852
(301) 897-5700

American Vocational Association
1410 King Street
Alexandria, VA 22314
(703) 683-3111

Association for Childhood Education International
17904 Georgia Avenue, Suite 215
Olney, MD 20832
(800) 423-3563

Association for Educational Communications and Technology
1025 Vermont Avenue, NW, Suite 820
Washington, D.C. 20005
(202) 347-7834

Association for Experiential Education
2305 Canyon Boulevard, Suite 100
Boulder, CO 80302
(303) 440-8844

Association for Gifted and Talented Students
228 Strauss Hall
Northeast LA University
Monroe, LA 71209
(318) 357-4572

Association for Supervision and Curriculum Development
1703 North Beauregard Street
Alexandria, VA 22311
(703) 578-9600

Council for Exceptional Children
1920 Association Drive
Reston, VA 22091
(703) 620-3660

Council for Learning Disabilities
P.O. Box 40303
Overland Park, KS 66204
(913) 492-8755

International Reading Association
800 Barksdale Road
P.O. Box 8139
Newark, DE 19714
(302) 731-1600

Kappa Delta Pi
1601 West State Street
P.O. Box 2669
West Lafayette, IN 47996-2669
(765) 743-1705

Learning Disabilities Association of America
4156 Library Road
Pittsburgh, PA 15234
(412) 341-1515

Lutheran Education Association
7400 Augusta
River Forest, IL 60305
(708) 209-3343

Modern Language Association
10 Astor Place
New York, NY 10003
(212) 475-9500

Music Teachers National Association
441 Vine Street, Suite 505
Cincinnati, OH 45202
(513) 421-1420

National Alliance of Black School Education
2816 Georgia Avenue, NW
Washington, D.C. 20001
(202) 483-1549

National Art Educators Association
1916 Association Drive
Reston, VA 22091
(703) 860-8000

National Association for Bilingual Education
1220 L Street, NW, Suite 605
Washington, D.C. 20005
(202) 898-1829

National Association of Biology Teachers
11250 Roger Bacon Drive, No. 19
Reston, VA 22090
(703) 471-1134

National Association of Elementary School
Principals
1615 Duke Street
Alexandria, VA 22314
(703) 684-3345

National Association for Gifted Children
1707 L Street NW, No. 550
Washington, D.C. 20036
(202) 785-4268

National Association for Industry-Education
Cooperation
235 Hendricks Boulevard
Buffalo, NY 14226
(716) 834-7047

National Association of School Psychologists
4340 East West Highway, Suite 402
Bethesda, MD 20814
(301) 657-0270

National Association of Secondary School
Principals
1904 Association Drive
Reston, VA 20190
(703) 860-0200

National Business Education Association
1914 Association Drive
Reston, VA 20191
(703) 860-8300

National Catholic Education Association
1077 30th Street NW, Suite 100
Washington, D.C. 20007
(202) 337-6232

National Council for the Social Studies
3501 Newark Street NW
Washington, D.C. 20016
(202) 966-7840

National Council of Teachers of English
1111 Kenyon Road
Urbana, IL 61801
(217) 328-3870

National Council of Teachers of Mathematics
1906 Association Drive
Reston, VA 20191
(703) 620-9840

National Education Association
1201 16th Street NW
Washington, D.C. 20036
(202) 833-4000

National Middle School Association
2600 Corporate Exchange Drive, Suite 370
Columbus, OH 43231
(614) 895-4730

National Rural Education Association
Colorado State University
230 Education Building
Fort Collins, CO 80523
(970)491-7022

National Science Teachers Association
1840 Wilson Boulevard
Arlington, VA 22201
(703) 243-7100

Phi Delta Kappa
4204 W. Robinwood Drive
Muncie, IN 47304
(765) 282-5462

Teachers of English to Speakers of Other
Languages
1600 Cameron Street, Suite 300
Alexandria, VA 22314
(703) 836-0774

School Supplies

Here is a general list of school supplies (consumable and non-consumable) that you might need. Create additional lists of supplies that you might need to teach the specific curriculum for your grade level or subject.

    H.1   Furniture:

           a. desks (students', teacher's, assistants')

           b. chairs (students', adults')

           c. tables

    H.2   Classroom Accessories:

           a. globe

           b. maps

           c. flannel board

           d. pocket chart

           e. chart paper easel, big book stand

           f. dictionary

           g. thesaurus

h. timers, bell

i. recess equipment (such as balls, jump ropes, and cones)

H.3 A/V Equipment:

a. projectors (overhead, slide, film)

b. television and VCR (with necessary cables)

c. filmstrip viewers

d. screen

e. extension cords

f. slides, films, videos, filmstrips

g. computers, printers, software

h. tape recorder

H.4 School Equipment:

a. keys to classroom, storage rooms

b. laminating machine

c. book binding machine

d. electric or heavy duty 3-hole punch

e. large paper cutter

f. photocopier, personalized key or code

g. die-cut machine for making bulletin board letters and shapes

H.5 "Office" Supplies:

a. lesson plan book

b. grade book (or software to do the same)

c. paper (plain copier, colored copier, lined notebook paper, newsprint, lined newsprint, construction, tissue, spiral and marble notebooks, printer, legal pads, notepads, chart, butcher, colored bulletin board)

d. regular and colored pencils, pens (black, blue, and colored), magic markers (washable and permanent), overhead transparency pens, dry-erase markers, crayons

e. pencil sharpener

f. erasers (pencil top, rectangular)

g. glue (white glue, rubber cement)

h. thumbtacks

i. stapler, staples, stapler remover

j. paper clips (all kinds and sizes)

k. scissors ("righty" and "lefty," adult and student sizes)

l.   rulers, yard sticks, meter sticks

m. rubber bands

n. tape (transparent, masking)

o. hole puncher (hand held, 3-hole punch)

p. chalk, whiteboard markers

q. overhead transparencies (for photocopier, for transparency maker, for just writing on)

r. chalkboard or whiteboard eraser

s. clipboard

t. envelopes

u. school stationary

v. file folders

w. hanging file folders

x. pocket folders

y. binders

z. divider inserts for three-ring binders

aa. safety pins

ab. stamp pads, stamps, ink

ac. craft supplies (such as pipe cleaners, felt, yarn, paint, and cloth)

ad. stickers and labels (folders, student awards)

ae. sticky note pads

af. blank audiocassettes, videotapes, computer diskettes

ag. printer cartridges

ah. toner for photocopying machines

H.6   Cleaning Supplies:

a. soap, cleansers, detergents

b. broom, mop, dustpan

c. buckets

d. paper towels

e. tissues

f. sponges

g. scrub brushes

h. rags

ERIC

ERIC is the Educational Resources Information Center, a federally funded, nationwide information network designed to provide educators with easy access to educational literature. The heart of ERIC is its database, the largest educational database in the world. The ERIC system is managed by the U.S. Department of Education's Office of Educational Research and Improvement (OERI). It consists of 16 clearinghouses. It also has additional support components, such as ERIC Document Reproduction Service (EDRS) and ACCESS ERIC which develops publications that help the public understand and use ERIC.

You can get access to ERIC from university libraries and from many public and professional libraries. You can also use a personal computer and the Internet to connect to ERIC. To obtain general information about ERIC and links to all ERIC Internet sites, start at the following ERIC system-wide site.

- URL: **http://www.accesseric.org:81**

If you do not have Internet access and need general information about ERIC, call ACCESS ERIC at **1-800-LET-ERIC (1-800-538-3742)** or send an e-mail message to **ericdb@aspensys.com**. Request their pocket guide to ERIC and a guide entitled *All About ERIC*. Both are excellent resources for understanding what ERIC has to offer and how to navigate through the database.

Special Days to Remember

Use the space provided to add any day that you would like to remember. For example, you might want to add a particular authors' birthday, a key historical event, or a nationally observed event such as National Book Week. Dates for these special days can be found in teacher prepared curriculum materials on the topics you are interested in.

July
4 - Independence Day

August
Friendship Day (1st Sun.)

September
Labor Day (1st Mon.)
National Grandparent's Day (1st Sun)
First Day of Autumn (3rd week)

October
31 - Halloween
Columbus Day (2nd Mon.)

November

11 - Veteran's Day
Election Day (1st Tues.)
Thanksgiving (4th Thurs.)
National Book Week (3rd week)

December

25 - Christmas
First Day of Winter (3rd week)
Hanukkah (date varies)

January

1 - New Year's Day
15 - Martin Luther King, Jr.'s Birthday
Chinese New Year (date varies)

February

2 - Ground Hog Day
12 - Abraham Lincoln's Birthday
22 - George Washington's Birthday
President's Day (3rd Mon.)

March

17 - St. Patrick's Day
First Day of Spring (3rd week)
Hobby Week (3rd week)
Health Week (last week)
Easter (or in April)
Passover (or in April)

April

22 - Earth Day Anniversary
National Arbor Day (last Fri.)
Easter (or in March)
Passover (or in March)

May

1 - May Day
5 - Cinco de Mayo
18 - Peace Day
Mother's Day (2nd Sun.)
Memorial Day (last Mon.)

June

14 - Flag Day
Father's Day (usually 3rd Sun.)
First Day of Summer (3rd week)

Bibliography

Bozzone, M. A. (1995, January-February). A teacher's stress survival guide. *Instructor*, pp. 55-57.

Cockburn, A. D. (1996). *Teaching under pressure*. London, England: Falmer Press.

Farber, B. A. (1991). *Crisis in education: Stress and burnout in the American teacher*. San Francisco, CA: Jossey-Bass.

Gold, Y., & Roth, R. A. (1993). *Teachers managing stress and preventing burnout: The professional health solution*. London, England: Falmer Press.

Grusko, R., & Kramer, J. (1993). *Becoming a teacher: A practical and political school survival guide*. Bloomington, IN: EDINFO Press.

Gupta, N. (1981). *Some sources and remedies of work stress among teachers*. Austin, TX: Southwest Educational Development Laboratory. (ERIC Document Reproduction Service No. ED 211 496).

Halpin, G., Harris, K., & Halpin, G. (1985). Teacher stress as related to locus of control, sex, and age. *Journal of Experimental Education*, *53*(3), 136-140.

Hoppenstedt, E. M., & Thomas, C. C. (1991). *A teacher's guide to classroom management*. Springfield, IL: Charles C Thomas.

Inlander, C. B., & Moran, Cynthia K. (1996). *Stress: 63 ways to relieve tension and stay healthy*. New York: Walker and Company.

Kabat-Zinn, J. (1990). *Full catastrophe living: Using the wisdom of your body and mind to face stress, pain, and illness*. New York: Delta.

Kronowitz, E. L. (1992). *Beyond student teaching*. White Plains, NY: Longman.

Kyriacou, C. (1987). Teacher stress and burnout: An international review. *Educational Research, 29*(2), 146-152.

Lombardi, J. D. (1995, January-February). Do you have teacher burnout? *Instructor*, pp. 64-65.

Megay-Nespoli, K. (1993). *The firt year for elementary school teachers: A practical plan for dealing with the short and long-term management of teaching duties and responsiblities*. Springfield, IL: Charles C Thomas.

McGrath, M. Z. (1995). *Teachers today: A guide to surviving creatively*. Thousand Oaks, CA: Corwin Press.

Miller, A. (1988, April 25). Stress on the job. *Newsweek*, pp. 40-45.

Moran, C., Stobbe, J., Baron, W., Miller, J., & Moir, E. (1992). *Keys to the classroom: A teacher's gruide to the first month of school*. Newbury Park, CA: Corwin Press.

Partin, R. L. (1995). *Classroom teacher's survival guide*. West Nyack, NY: The Center for Applied Research in Education.

Powell, J. R. (1994). *The working woman's guide to managing stress*. Englewood Cliffs, NJ: Prentice Hall.

Scaros, B. C. (1981). *Sight on sites: an approach to coping with teacher stress— preventing burn-out*. New York: New York City Teacher Centers Consortium. (ERIC Document Reproduction Service No. ED 236 131).

Selye, H. (1974). *Stress without distress*. New York: The New American Library.

Shalaway, L. (1989). *Learning to teach: Not just for beginners*. New York: Scholastic.

Steere, B. F. (1988). *Becoming an effective classroom manager: A resource for teachers*. Albany, NY: State University of New York Press.

Swick, K. J. (1989). *Stress and teaching*. Washington, D. C.: National Education Association.

Swick, K. J. (1987). *Student stress: A classroom management system*. Washington, D. C.: National Education Association.

Warner, J., & Bryan, C. (1995). *The unauthorized teacher's survival guide*. Indianapolis, IN: Park Avenue Publications.

Williamson, B. (1993). *A first-year teacher's guidebook for success* (rev. ed.). Sacramento, CA: Dynamic Teaching Co.

Wilson-Brown, G. (1994). *The assertive teacher*. Hants, England: Arena.

Index

Notes

Order Form

Products:

EL-99160 7 Steps to Stress Free Teaching: A Stress Prevention Planning Guide for Teachers $19.95
EL-99096 7 Steps to Stress Free Teaching Plan Book $9.95

Please send the following books:

Item No.	Title	Quantity	Unit Price	Total Price

Subtotal:	
Sales Tax:	
Shipping:	
Total:	

Sales Tax: NC residents add 6% sales tax.
Shipping: $3.00 for the first book and $2.00 each additional book.
Payment: Make checks payable to Educators' Lighthouse.

Volume discounts apply. Call or write for details.

Ship order to:

Name:

Address:

City: State: Zip:

Telephone:

Mail order with payment to:
Educators' Lighthouse
5133 Fairmead Circle
Raleigh, NC 27613

EDUCATORS' LIGHTHOUSE

5133 Fairmead Circle, Raleigh, NC 27613
tel: 919-848-2058
fax: 919-846-9084
toll free: 800-567-0310